Kiera Clayton Travel Guide To

OBAN

SCOTLAND

Tourist comprehensive details and useful advice

KIERA CLAYTON

COPYRIGHT NOTICE

No part of this publication may be reproduced, distributed, or transmitted in any form or by any means, including photocopying, recording, or other electronic or mechanical methods, without the prior written permission of the Author, except in the case of brief quotations embodied in critical reviews and certain other non-commercial uses permitted by copyright law.

DISCLAIMER

The information provided in this publication is intended for educational purposes only. It has been sourced from materials believed to be reliable at the time of publication. However, the opinions and information contained herein are subject to change without prior notice.

Readers acknowledge that the Author/Publisher is not offering legal, financial, or professional advice. The Publisher/Author makes no guarantees as to the accuracy, completeness, or adequacy of the information provided.

The Publisher assumes no responsibility for any errors, omissions, or misinterpretations of the information presented. The Publisher/Author expressly disclaims liability for any consequences arising from the use or application of the material contained in this book.

TABLE OF CONTENTS

Copyright Notice 2

Disclaimer 3

TABLE OF CONTENTS 4

INTRODUCTION 13

WELCOME TO OBAN 13

About This Travel Guide 14

Why Oban? 15

How To Use This Guide 17

CHAPTER 1 19

INTRODUCTION TO OBAN 19

Overview Of Oban 20

History Of Oban 20

Geography And Climate 21

Culture And Tradition 22

CHAPTER 2 24

PLANNING YOUR TRIP 24

Best Time To Visit 24

How To Get To Oban 26

Getting Around Oban 28

Accommodation Options...................................... 30

Selecting The Right Accommodation 31

CHAPTER 3 34

ACCOMMODATION IN OBAN 34

Overview Of Accommodation Options 34

Luxury Resorts 37

Budget-Friendly Hotels 39

Boutique Guesthouse 41

Unique Stays.. 44

Top Recommended Accommodation 46

Selecting The Suitable Accommodation 48

Booking Tips And Tricks....................................... 50

CHAPTER 4 53

OUTDOOR activities IN OBAN 53

Cruise To The Isles 53

Hiking Trails.. 55

Sea Kayaking 57

Wildlife Watching 59

CHAPTER 5 62

DINING AND CULINARY EXPERIENCES 62

    Seafood Restaurants 63

    Traditional Scottish Fare 65

    Cafes And Bakeries 67

    Whisky Tasting 69

    CHAPTER 6 72

SHOPPING IN OBAN 72

    Souvenir Shops 72

    Local Markets..74

    Craft Boutiques...75

    Specialty Stores 77

    CHAPTER 7 80

DAY TRIPS FROM OBAN 80

    Island Of Mull 80

    Isle Of Staffa 82

    Glencoe...83

    Inveraray 84

    CHAPTER 8 87

FESTIVALS AND EVENTS IN OBAN 87

    Oban Winter Festival 87

Highland Games 89

Oban Live Music Festival 91

Highland Cattle Show 92

CHAPTER 9 95

FAMILY-FRIENDLY ACTIVITIES.............................. 95

Sea Life Sanctuary 95

Paddleboard Lessons 97

Oban Chocolate Company 98

Oban Bay Play 100

CHAPTER 10 102

NIGHTLIFE IN OBAN 102

Pubs And Bars 102

Live Music Venues.. 104

Whisky Bars.. 105

Nightclubs.. 107

CHAPTER 11 109

WELLNESS AND RELAXATION................................ 109

Spa Retreats 109

Yoga Studios 111

Outdoor Wellness Activities 112

Wellness Workshops 113

CHAPTER 12 115

LOCAL ETIQUETTE AND CUSTOMS 115

Greeting And Politeness 116

Tipping Practices 117

Dinner Etiquette 118

Social Norms 119

CHAPTER 13 121

LEARNING BASIC SCOTISH GAELIC 121

Essential Gaelic Phrases 122

Language-Learning Resources 123

Cultural Etiquette Tips 125

Language Assistance Services 126

CHAPTER 14 129

ITINERARIES AND SAMPLE PLANS 129

Weekend Getaway 129

Cultural Immersion 133

Outdoor Adventure 137

Family-Friendly Trip 141

Budget Travel 145

Solo Traveler's Guide.. 148

Romantic Getaways 151

CHAPTER 15 155

SAFETY TIPS FOR VISITORS 155

General Safety Precautions... 155

Emergency Contacts.. 157

Health Care Facilities 158

Travel Insurance And Documents... 159

CHAPTER 16 162

SUSTAINABLE TRAVEL IN OBAN 162

Environmentally Friendly Accommodation Options........... 162

Responsible Tourist Practices.. 164

Conservation Efforts 166

Community Initiatives 167

CHAPTER 17 170

PHOTOGRAPHY GUIDE 170

Best Photospots.. 170

Lighting And Composition Tips... 172

Equipment Recommendations... 173

Editing And Post-Processing Techniques 174

-9-

CHAPTER 18 177

INSIDER TIPS FROM LOCALS 177

    Hidden Gems 178

    Off-Beaten Path Attractions 179

    Local Dining Secrets 180

    Insider Recommendations 181

CHAPTER 19..183
HISTORICAL AND CULTURAL WALKING TOURS 183

    Oban City Walking Tour 184

    Castle And Clan Tour 185

    Whisky Trail Tour 187

    Coastal Heritage Tour 188

    CHAPTER 20 191

EXPLORING OBAN'S LANDMARK...............................191

    McCaig's Tower 191

    Oban Distillery...192

    Dunollie Castle 194

    Oban War And Peace Museum 194

    CHAPTER 21 197

ACCOMMODATION AND DINING DIRECTORIES 197

Addresses And Locations For Popular Accommodation...... 197

Addresses And Locations Of Popular Restaurants And Cafés 199

Addresses And locations Of Popular Bars And Clubs 200

Addresses And Locations Of Major Attractions 202

CHAPTER 22 206

CONCLUSION 206

Reflecting On Your Oban Experience 206

Farewell Traditions In Oban 207

Plan Your Next Adventure 208

Leave Oban With Memories To Cherish............................. 208

CHAPTER 23 210

APPENDIX 210

Emergency Contacts.. 210

Maps And Navigational Tools.. 211

Additional Reading And References 212

Useful Local Phrases.. 213

Addresses And Locations Of Popular Accommodation 214

Addresses And Locations Of Popular Restaurants And Cafés 215

Addresses And Locations Of Popular Bars And Clubs 216

Addresses And Locations Of Top Attractions......................217

MAPS...219

Oban Scotland 219

Things To Do In Oban..220

Hotels In Oban...221

Vacation Rentals...222

Restaurants In Oban 223

Museums In Oban..224

Pharmacies In Oban...225

ATMs In Oban...226

Streets In Oban 227

Streets In Oban 228

Hiking Trails In Oban...229

IMAGE ATTRIBUTION..230
APPRECIATION..231

INTRODUCTION

WELCOME TO OBAN

Greetings, the stunning place you are about to see is the coastal village of Oban. Oban is a picturesque town in the west coast of Scotland that is famous for its stunning views, historical past and versatility. In fact, you can always find something in Oban; whether it is a gorgeous waterfront throughout, historical buildings or palaces, or delicious seafood.

When you are en-route to Oban, there is much to enjoy, from jagged coastline to lush inclines. The atmosphere of the town is friendly to newly arriving characters and offers good taverns, no rush in the daily life.

Oban's bustling harbor is the entryway to the Inner Hebrides, making it a popular destination for island hopping and exploring the beautiful islands of Mull, Iona, and Staffa. However, Oban is more than just a starting point for island excursions; it is a destination in its own right, with a plethora of sites, activities, and experiences waiting to be found.

About This Travel Guide

This tourist book is one of the most essential resources to use when visiting Oban and the surrounding regions. It is written with utmost confidentiality as a guide and manual, it is designed to provide the visitors with valuable tips, comprehensive details and useful advise to have an enjoyable and pleasant stay in Oban.

What You'll Find In This Guide

- Complete coverage of Oban's attractions, landmarks, and hidden secrets.
- Insider tips on food, shopping, nightlife, and outdoor activities.
- Practical information about transit, lodging options, and safety precautions.
- Cultural insights, historical background, and local etiquette advice will help you better understand and appreciate Oban.

- Sample itineraries and suggested strategies to help you make the most of your time and create lasting memories.

It doesn't matter if you're a first-time visitor or a seasoned traveler, this guide will help you organize the ideal trip to Oban and make the most of your Scottish journey.

Why Oban?

You might be wondering why Oban is a perfect destination for your next trip. Stunning Scenery.

Here are a few reasons why you should put Oban at the top of your bucket list:

Stunning Scenery: Oban is bordered by some of the most scenic regions of Scotland which is mountainous and includes peaceful lochs. The views of the port and neighboring islands are just breathtaking, particularly around sunset.

Rich History: Oban has therefore been through many transformations from pre-historic times. Learn about the town's historical background and check out McCaig's Tower,

Dunollie Castle, and Oban War and Peace Memorial and Museums.

Culinary Delights: Food is a popular aspect in Oban with fresh seafood, locally available meals and Scottish recipes. Take a bite of Grimsby's famous fish and chips, or perhaps haggis and black pudding, and of course do not forgo a visit to the famous Oban Distillery and whisky.

Outdoor Adventures: If you're a thrill-seeker or a nature lover, Oban has a variety of outdoor activities to suit your preferences. There are numerous activities available in and around Oban, including hiking, kayaking, animal watching, and boat cruises.

Warm Hospitality: One of the delights of visiting Oban is the friendly reception you'll receive from the inhabitants. Oban residents are known for their friendliness and hospitality, and they are always eager to share their enthusiasm for their hometown and provide insider advice to help you make the most of your visit.

How To Use This Guide

Navigating a new destination might be difficult, but do not worry—this guide is here to help!

Here's how to get the most out of this trip guide.

Navigation: The table of contents allows you to effortlessly move between chapters and locate the information you're looking for. Whether you're planning your trip, looking for restaurant recommendations, or looking for practical advice, everything is neatly categorized for quick access.

Insider Tips: Look for insider information and recommendations throughout the guide. These insider tips from residents and experienced travelers will help you find hidden jewels, avoid tourist traps, and make the most of your time in Oban.

Practical Information: Pay close attention to the practical information sections for important details on transit, lodging, safety tips, and more. These ideas will help you organize your journey and navigate Oban's streets with ease.

Example Itineraries: Look through the example itineraries and suggested strategies to help you organize your time in Oban.

By following these suggestions and using the materials in this book, you'll be well-prepared to confidently navigate Oban, immerse yourself in its culture and history, and make great memories of your Scottish vacation.

So, pack your luggage, tie up your hiking boots, and prepare to discover everything Oban has to offer!

CHAPTER 1

INTRODUCTION TO OBAN

Oban, often referred to as the 'the Seafood Capital of Scotland' or the 'Gateway to the Isles,' is a charismatic coastal town located in Scotland. Through its scenic beauty, historical background, and culture in showcasing tourism attractions, Oban continues to be the perfect place for anybody who is interested in an adventure, enjoys tranquility, or is on a discovery mission.

In this chapter, you will find a brief description of Oban, as well as the historical background of the place, and information about the climate and geographical features of the location, traditions, and customs of Oban.

Overview Of Oban

Oban is a popular resort town in the Argyll and Bute council area of Scotland on the west coast at the southern end of the Firth of Lorn. It is the most populous town in the region and plays a central role as a transport center with the mainland Scotland and the Inner Hebrides. Surprisingly, even this small town boasts a bustling harbor, beautiful narrow streets with shops and cafes, and remarkable views of the rocky shores.

Tourism forms the backbone of the economy in Oban, as people flock to the town to explore the historic buildings, taste the seafood delicacies, and engage in fishing, whisky production, as well as visiting nearby islands and attractions. Self-drive, cultural centres, wildlife, history, food and drinks are just some of the features that Oban has to offer.

History Of Oban

Evolution of Oban as the area can be dated back to the Mesolithic age although there is evidence of people inhabiting the area from thousands of years ago. Nonetheless, the modern town began to form in the 18th century Owing to its favorable position along the western coast of Scotland, it became a center for trade.

The arrival of railway in Oban in middle of nineteenth century was a turning point in the growth of the town as it became one of the most popular tourist destination. People from Glasgow and other parts of the world came to visit Oban to enjoy its natural beauty and seashore attractions, prompting the establishment of hotels, guesthouses, and other tourist amenities.

Oban saw wealth and growth during the Victorian era, with the creation of notable landmarks like McCaig's Tower, a stunning coliseum-style edifice that overlooks the town. Oban's rich history is now represented in its architecture, museums, and cultural heritage, offering visitors an intriguing peek into the past.

Geography And Climate

The geography of Oban is also very diverse with steep beach fronts, hilly grounds, and eye appealing islands. The town is set amidst stunning views including the Ben Lui and Ben Cruachan ranges or the coastal view of the panorama.

The climate in Oban is relatively warm and it receives reasonable rainfall because it is located on the coastal region. Summer is often warm and sunny there, and the climate is very good for outdoor activities like hiking, kayaking, and wildlife viewing. Cooler temperatures are experienced during winter despite the fact that Oban does not experience very cold or snowy weather making this season ideal for visits.

Culture And Tradition

Thus, the cultural background of Oban can be considered rather rich and formed by the Gaelic origin of its inhabitants, marine traditions, and strong community spirit. Its links with the Gaelic culture can be evidenced by the use of Gaelic names for different places in the town, local music, and themed occasions including Highland Games and Oban's Live Music festival.

The Highland Games, a centuries-old sporting event featuring traditional Scottish games such as caber tossing, hammer throwing, and Highland dancing, are one of Oban's most treasured traditions. The games draw athletes and spectators from all over the world and are a high point on the town's cultural calendar.

The town is also popular for its music arena with live music entertainment throughout the year in the town's bars, restaurants and concert halls. Doubtless, many guests like traditional folk, but the town attracts fans of modern rock and pop music as well.

Beyond the culture and traditions, Oban is famous for its seafood food that uses fish caught from the Firth of Lorn on the same day. Some of the locally sourced produce include Oban Bay oysters, West Coast scallops, freshly landed langoustines are among the local delicacies available in restaurants and seafood shacks throughout town.

Overall, Oban's culture and customs reflect its rich history, stunning landscapes, and spirit of togetherness, which captures both near and distant guests with a friendly disposition and fabulous experience.

CHAPTER 2

PLANNING YOUR TRIP

Planning for a trip to Oban involves choosing appropriate time to visit the destination, getting transport and an accommodation.

This chapter provides you with essential information that will assist you in preparing for your visit to Oban and ensure that you enjoy your stay in this beautiful sea-side town.

Best Time To Visit

The best time to pay a visit to Oban depends on your preferences because each season is different and there are always new experiences to enjoy in the town. The following article explains the various seasons and what you are likely to experience at certain times of the year.

Spring (March To May): It is recommended that one should visit Oban in the spring since the countryside comes alive with beautiful flowers and green vegetation. The climate is generally mild warm months which is good for hiking, sighting animals and viewing attractions within the town. Also, tourism is usually at a low figure in Spring as compared to summer tourism, implying that you may be able to get a booking at a much lesser rate than you would in the middle of summer.

Summer (June To August): is considered the peak season as the temperature is high, days are longer, and the calendar is full of events and activities in Oban. During this season, the town bustles with activities such as festivals, outdoor concerts, and cultural activities therefore making the town to attract many tourists. However, anticipate that there will be more people present and the prices especially in hotels and tour companies will be higher. To secure your preferred dates, reserve your lodgings and activities early.

Autumn (September To November): Traveling to Oban in the autumn is always a good idea since the countryside becomes colorful in shades of red, orange, and gold. The climate remains moderate, which is perfect for out-door activities such as hiking, cycling, and driving around. Autumn also brings the possibility of joining the town's harvest celebrations and cuisine fairs where you can taste delicious treats and fresh picked vegetables.

Winter (December To February): Oban is calmer than the high tourist season, yet it has its own distinct attractions. While the weather cools, the town becomes more festive, with crackling fires and warm hospitality. Winter is a great time to visit indoor sites like museums, galleries, and whisky distilleries, as well as eat hearty Scottish comfort food at local pubs and restaurants.

Finally, the optimum time to visit Oban is determined by your personal interests and preferences. Oban offers lots to offer all year, whether you're looking for outdoor adventures, cultural events, or just a quiet break.

How To Get To Oban

Oban is easily accessible via several kinds of transportation, including:

By Car: Oban is accessible by road transport and if you are coming from Glasgow or Edinburgh it is advisable that you drive to Oban. It takes about 2-3 hours by car from Glasgow and 3-4 hours when traveling from Edinburgh, provided that there is free traffic.

The main road accesses to Oban are the A82 and A85 roads and are scenic drives through the rural Scottish landscape.

By Train: Another option is a train, which can be taken from Glasgow Queen Street Station to Oban. ScotRail offers daily services to Oban and the journey can take anything between 3 hours and 30 minutes. The train ride exposes some of the most famous parts of Scotland and is considered one of the most beautiful Railway routes in the country..

By Bus: Many companies offer bus services to Oban from all over Scotland and other big cities and towns. There are many buses provided by Citylink from Glasgow and Edinburgh to Oban and there is more than one bus provided in a day. The bus takes about between 3 and 4 hours from Glasgow and between 4 and 5 hours from Edinburgh.

By Ferry: Caledonian MacBrayne (CalMac) provides ferry service to Oban from the Inner Hebrides islands and other coastal communities. The ferry station is near the town center, making it easy to get to Oban's sights and amenities once you arrive.

By Air: At present there is no airport in Oban However, the closest airports include Glasgow and Edinburgh airports where local and international flights are available. To reach Oban from airports, you can either take a car rental service, go by rail or bus, or arrange a private transfer.

Getting Around Oban

After getting into Oban, it becomes easy and convenient to move around since the town is well mapped out. The main central business district of the town is not very large, and hence, major attractions in the town can be explored on foot:

Walking: This includes crosswalks and sidewalks and safe pedestrian streets for Oban's town center. Most of the attractions, shops, restaurants, and accommodations are in close proximity to one another and you can walk around freely to enjoy the ambiance of Oban.

Local Buses: West Coast Motors provides local bus services in and around Oban, connecting to adjacent villages, attractions, and picturesque sites. Bus stops are scattered around the town, and the fares are reasonable, making it a convenient way to move around.

Taxis: Taxis are widely available in Oban and can be hailed on the street or reserved in advance. Taxi ranks can be found near the ferry port, rail station, and in the town center. Taxis are a useful way to go short distances or outside of the town center.

Car Rentals: If you intend to explore the surrounding area or travel further afield, hiring a car is a practical alternative. Several car rental companies have locations in Oban and offer a variety of automobiles to meet your demands and budget. Having your own vehicle allows you to explore at your own speed and reach remote locations that may not be accessible via public transportation.

Cycling: Cycling is a popular way to explore Oban and the surrounding countryside, with attractive routes and paths appropriate for riders of all skill levels. Bring your own bike or hire one from one of the town's bike shops.

Accommodation Options

Oban has a wide range of accommodation alternatives to suit every budget and preference, including luxurious hotels, quaint guesthouses, bed & breakfasts, and self-catering flats.

Here are some of the lodging possibilities in Oban:

Hotels: Oban has a variety of hotels, ranging from luxurious facilities with beachfront views to more affordable options in the town center. Whether you're looking for a boutique hotel with chic decor or a family-friendly resort with onsite amenities, you'll have plenty of options.

Guesthouses And Bed And Breakfasts: If you want a more private and customized experience, stay at an Oban guesthouse or bed and breakfast. These beautiful hotels are frequently managed by friendly hosts who may offer insider information and suggestions for visiting the area.

Self-Catering Apartments: If you want more freedom and independence during your stay, self-catering apartments are an excellent choice. These fully furnished apartments include kitchens or kitchenettes, so you can prepare your own meals and have a home-away-from-home experience in Oban.

Hostels: Hostels are plans for budget-conscious tourists as they offer facilities such as dormitories, bar, TV lounge, and kitchenette at cheap rates. It is a good practice to interact with other guests and to exchange contact information and other tips related to Oban's attractions as well as travelling further afield.

Campsites And Caravan Parks: For those, who are in search of a more outdoor experience, Oban and its loch side surroundings has numerous opportunities for camping and caravan sites. It may range from finding a small, flat space for putting up a tent to towing your caravan or motor home into a beautiful pastoral landscape – or even finding campsites with relatively contemporary facilities.

Selecting The Right Accommodation

Deciding on the kind of lodging to take while in Oban depends on your interests, pocket and way of travels.

Here are some things to bear in mind:

Location: Decide whether you want to book a hotel in the heart of the town, proximal to water bodies or inland, outside the city. While choosing the accommodation, look at the proximity of the hotel to various sights, eateries, and varieties of transport systems.

Amenities: Consider what other aspects are important to you, from dining out, to parking, to free Internet, to amenities like fitness centers and swimming pools, to spas, and so on. Select a hotel with facilities and services that will complement your visit to Oban.

Budget: Establish a budget for your lodging and hunt for possibilities that are within your pricing range. Remember that rates can change based on the time of year, so be flexible with your travel dates if feasible.

Reviews And Ratings: When looking for accommodation, always look at the experiences of other guests who have stayed previously in order to get an idea of the overall quality of the service. Select hotels with customer reviews as positive as possible especially in terms of cleanliness, comfort and friendliness of the staff.

Special Offers And Packages: Look at any additional bonus offers, promotions, or lower price options concerning your chosen hotel. Most of the hotels and guesthouses offered several offerings such as advance booking discount, multiple night stay and out of season bookings.

Accessibility: If you have any special requirements for the accommodation, or if you have problems with your mobility, please do not hesitate to ask about the availability of the ramps, lifts and specially equipped rooms at the time of your booking.

In conclusion, choosing the right among the numerous hotels is a crucial step in planning your trip to Oban and the choice can significantly affect your impressions.

Oban has a variety of options to suit any traveler's needs and interests, from luxurious hotels with breathtaking views to quiet guesthouses with a personal touch.

CHAPTER 3

ACCOMMODATION IN OBAN

When planning your trip to Oban, selecting the proper accommodations is critical to ensure a pleasant and happy experience. Oban provides a broad choice of lodging alternatives to meet the interests and preferences of every traveler, from luxurious resorts to intimate bed and breakfasts.

In this chapter, we will look at the many types of accommodation available in Oban and offer advice on how to choose the best location to stay during your visit.

Overview Of Accommodation Options

Oban has a diverse choice of lodging alternatives to suit varied budgets, preferences, and travel patterns. Oban has a wide range of lodging options, including luxury resorts with spectacular views, charming guesthouses with personalized service, and budget-friendly hostels for a low-cost stay.

Here's a summary of the kinds of accommodations available:

Hotels: Oban has a variety of hotels, ranging from premium facilities with beachfront views to more affordable options in the town center. Hotels include a variety of amenities, including onsite dining, fitness centers, and concierge services, making them perfect for travelers looking for comfort and convenience.

Guesthouses And Bed And Breakfasts: If you want a more private and customized experience, stay at an Oban guesthouse or bed and breakfast. These beautiful hotels are frequently managed by friendly hosts who may offer insider information and suggestions for visiting the area. Guests can enjoy pleasant lodgings, homemade breakfasts, and a warm Scottish welcome.

Self-Catering Apartments: Self-catering flats are a popular choice for guests who want flexibility and independence during their stay. These completely furnished apartments include kitchens or kitchenettes, allowing guests to prepare their own meals and enjoy a home-away-from-home atmosphere in Oban. Self-catering apartments are great for families, groups, and travelers planning a long-term visit.

Hostels: Budget-conscious tourists might find economical lodging alternatives in Oban. Hostels provide dormitory-style rooms with shared amenities, as well as individual rooms for people who prefer more privacy. Hostels are an excellent opportunity to meet other visitors and share advice and recommendations for visiting Oban and beyond.

Campsites And Caravan Parks: For outdoor enthusiasts, Oban and its neighboring surroundings include a variety of campsites and caravan parks. Whether you want to pitch a tent under the stars or park your caravan in a picturesque spot, you'll discover campsites with modern amenities and stunning natural surroundings. Camping is an excellent opportunity to connect with nature and participate in outdoor activities such as hiking, fishing, and wildlife watching.

Regardless of your budget or tastes, Oban has accommodations to meet every traveler's demand and ensure a great stay in this picturesque seaside town.

Luxury Resorts

Luxury resorts in Oban provide the best in comfort, with unsurpassed amenities, breathtaking vistas, and great service.

It doesn't matter if you're celebrating a special occasion or simply looking for a deluxe weekend, these resorts offer a break from the ordinary and the opportunity to explore Oban in style. Here are some of the best luxury resorts in Oban:

The Manor House Hotel: Nestled in lush gardens overlooking Oban Bay, provides elegant accommodations, fine cuisine, and a variety of leisure amenities. Guests can repose in spacious rooms and suites with modern facilities, eat in the hotel's award-winning restaurant, and relax in the spa and wellness center.

Perle Oban Hotel: Perle Oban Hotel, located in the heart of Oban's town center, provides boutique accommodations with contemporary style and breathtaking views of the bay. The hotel offers elegant rooms and suites with luxurious furniture, an onsite restaurant providing locally sourced cuisine, and a rooftop terrace with panoramic views of the surrounding area.

Isle Of Eriska Hotel: Located on a private island off the coast of Oban, the Isle of Eriska Hotel provides a tranquil refuge surrounded by natural beauty. Guests can choose between magnificent apartments and suites in the historic main house and private cottages dotted throughout the estate. The hotel boasts a Michelin-starred restaurant, a golf course, a spa, and outdoor activities including hiking, fishing, and animal watching.

Airds Hotel And Restaurant: Located in the scenic village of Port Appin, just a short drive from Oban, Airds Hotel and Restaurant provides luxurious rooms in a peaceful environment. Guests can relax in individually built rooms and suites, enjoy gourmet meals made with locally sourced ingredients, and explore the surrounding countryside on guided walks and outdoor experiences.

Knipoch Hotel: Located in a historic country home surrounded by acres of beautiful grounds, the Knipoch Hotel provides a tranquil respite from the rush and bustle of everyday life. Guests can enjoy elegant accommodations, traditional Scottish cuisine, and friendly service in a gorgeous setting overlooking Loch Feochan.

These luxury resorts in Oban offer the ideal balance of elegance, comfort, and relaxation, allowing guests to immerse themselves in the majesty of Scotland's west coast while enjoying world-class amenities and outstanding service.

Budget-Friendly Hotels

Travelers on a budget will discover a variety of economical lodging options in Oban, including budget-friendly hotels that provide comfort and convenience without breaking the bank. These hotels offer basic amenities and decent rooms at reasonable prices, making them ideal for budget-conscious tourists wishing to explore Oban and the surrounding areas without going overboard.

Here are some cost-effective hotels in Oban:

Oban Bay Hotel And Spa: Located on the waterfront promenade, the Oban Bay Hotel and Spa provides economical lodging with breathtaking views of Oban Bay. The hotel has comfortable rooms with modern facilities, an onsite restaurant featuring Scottish cuisine, and a spa that offers a variety of treatments and therapies. Guests have convenient access to the town center, ferry station, and nearby attractions.

Regent Hotel: Located in the heart of Oban's town center, Regent Hotel provides affordable lodgings in a convenient position. The hotel offers comfortable rooms with en-suite bathrooms, free Wi-Fi, and flat-screen televisions. The hotel's onsite restaurant and bar serves hearty Scottish breakfasts and traditional pub meals.

Columba Hotel: Overlooking Oban Bay, the Columba Hotel provides cheap accommodations with breathtaking views of the harbor and surrounding mountains. The hotel offers pleasant rooms with en-suite bathrooms, satellite television, and tea/coffee making facilities. Guests can dine at the hotel's restaurant, which serves a variety of Scottish and foreign cuisine, or unwind with a drink in the lounge bar.

Lancaster Hotel: Located within walking distance of Oban's town center, the Lancaster Hotel provides affordable lodgings in a handy position. The motel offers modest rooms with en-suite bathrooms, free Wi-Fi, and flat-screen televisions. Every morning, guests can have a full Scottish breakfast before relaxing in the hotel's pleasant lounge area.

St. Anne's Guest House: Located in a residential neighborhood just a short walk from Oban's town center, St. Anne's Guest House provides economical lodging in a delightful Victorian property. The guesthouse offers comfortable rooms with en-suite bathrooms, flat-screen TVs, and free Wi-Fi. Every morning, guests can have a superb breakfast in the dining room before exploring the town's attractions on foot.

These low-cost hotels in Oban offer comfortable lodgings, handy services, and outstanding value for money, making them ideal for those looking for inexpensive options during their stay to this lovely coastal town.

Boutique Guesthouse

Boutique guesthouses in Oban provide one-of-a-kind accommodations with elegant décor, excellent service, and a warm setting for guests wanting a more private and personal experience. These boutique properties frequently have specially decorated rooms, gourmet breakfasts, and unique touches that make for an unforgettable visit.

Here are several boutique guest homes in Oban:

Roseneath Guest House: Set in a historic Victorian building overlooking Oban Bay, Roseneath Guest House provides boutique lodgings with lovely decor and modern conveniences. The guest home offers specially designed rooms with exquisite furnishings, Egyptian cotton sheets, and complimentary toiletries. Every morning, guests can have a delicious breakfast in the dining room or unwind in the pleasant lounge area with spectacular views of the bay.

Glenrigh Guest House: Located in a quiet residential neighborhood just a short walk from Oban's town center, Glenrigh Guest House provides boutique lodgings in a peaceful environment. The guesthouse has tastefully fitted rooms with contemporary décor, luxurious linen, and quality toiletries. Guests can begin their day with a freshly prepared breakfast made from locally sourced ingredients before relaxing in the guest lounge or garden terrace.

Braeside Guest House: Located in the lovely village of Connel, just outside of Oban, Braeside Guest House provides boutique lodgings and a warm Scottish welcome. The guest house has attractive rooms decorated with vintage furniture, original artwork, and modern comforts. Each morning, guests can enjoy a delicious breakfast in the dining room or unwind in the pleasant guest lounge, which features a selection of novels, games, and DVDs.

Sutherland Guest House: Nestled in a quiet residential neighborhood overlooking Oban Bay, Sutherland Guest House provides boutique accommodations with breathtaking views and customized service. The guest house offers beautifully furnished rooms with quality bedding, fluffy bathrobes, and complimentary refreshments. Guests can unwind in the guest lounge or garden terrace, eat a great breakfast every morning, and get insider insights and recommendations from the kind hosts.

These Oban boutique guesthouses provide a one-of-a-kind and memorable experience, with individualized service, beautiful lodgings, and meticulous attention to detail that will make your visit truly special. Whether you're celebrating a special occasion or just looking for a comfortable escape, these boutique resorts offer the ideal environment for a relaxing vacation in Oban.

Unique Stays

Oban provides a variety of unique lodgings that go beyond standard hotels and guesthouses for those looking for a one-of-a-kind experience. These one-of-a-kind lodgings, ranging from historic castles and lighthouses to cozy cottages and luxury glamping sites, make Oban a remarkable destination.

Here are some unique accommodations to consider:

Barcaldine Castle: Perched on a hill overlooking Loch Creran, Barcaldine Castle provides an amazing experience in a medieval environment. This restored castle from the 16th century boasts magnificent rooms with antique furnishings, four-poster beds, and breathtaking views of the surrounding landscape. Guests can have afternoon tea in the castle's drawing room, wander the gardens, or unwind by the fireplace in the great hall.

Easdale Island Bunkhouse: For a one-of-a-kind island retreat, visit the calm island of Easdale and stay at the Easdale Island Bunkhouse. This eco-friendly bunkhouse provides basic lodgings in a former slate quarry structure, with dormitory-style rooms, communal kitchen facilities, and magnificent views of the surrounding sea and islands. Guests can explore the island's rough coastline, visit the Easdale Island Folk Museum, or take a boat to neighboring islands.

Oban Bay Yurt: The Oban Bay Yurt offers a unique glamping experience on a hillside overlooking Oban Bay. This traditional Mongolian yurt provides pleasant accommodations, with a wood-burning stove, comfortable furnishings, and a private deck with stunning views. Guests can relax in the surrounding countryside, take walks in the neighboring forests, or stare at the stars from the outdoor hot tub.

Kilchurn Castle Lodge: Stay at a beautiful lodge just steps away from the historic Kilchurn Castle on Loch Awe's shoreline. This refurbished lodge provides pleasant accommodations with modern conveniences such as a fully outfitted kitchen, large sitting areas, and outdoor lounging areas overlooking the castle ruins. Guests can explore the castle grounds, fish in the lake, or go for lovely walks along the shoreline.

Kerrera Bunkhouse: Escape to the isolated island of Kerrera and stay at the Kerrera Bunkhouse for a relaxing escape surrounded by nature. This eco-friendly bunkhouse provides modest accommodations in a converted farm building, complete with dormitory-style rooms, community kitchen facilities, and breathtaking views of the surrounding countryside. Guests can explore the island's walking trails, see the remnants of Gylen Castle, or simply relax and unwind in the peaceful surroundings.

These one-of-a-kind Oban accommodations provide an unforgettable experience, letting guests to immerse themselves in the natural beauty, history, and charm of Scotland's countryside.

Top Recommended Accommodation

With so many accommodation options in Oban, it might be difficult to find the ideal location to stay. To help you narrow down your options, here are some top-rated Oban lodgings based on user reviews, amenities, and overall experience:

The Manor House Hotel: Located on the seaside promenade, The Manor House Hotel provides magnificent accommodations, fine cuisine, and a variety of recreational amenities. Guests compliment the hotel's gorgeous setting, attentive service, and spacious rooms with breathtaking views of Oban Bay.

Roseneath Guest House: Roseneath Guest House, which overlooks Oban Bay, provides boutique lodgings with attractive décor and modern conveniences. Guests remark about the guest house's friendly staff, delectable breakfasts, and breathtaking views of the bay.

Oban Bay Hotel And Spa: Located on the waterfront promenade, the Oban Bay Hotel and Spa provides economical lodging with breathtaking views of Oban Bay. Guests enjoy the hotel's convenient location, courteous staff, and on-site spa facilities.

Perle Oban Hotel: Perle Oban Hotel, located in the heart of Oban's town center, provides boutique accommodations with contemporary style and magnificent views of the port. The hotel's elegant accommodations, great restaurant, and rooftop terrace with views of the town are all popular with guests.

Barcaldine Castle: Perched atop a hill overlooking Loch Creran, provides a unique and remarkable experience in a medieval setting. Guests laud the castle's luxury lodgings, breathtaking vistas, and excellent service.

These top-rated Oban lodgings have garnered excellent ratings from guests for their exceptional service, pleasant accommodations, and handy locations.

Even if you're looking for luxury, boutique charm, or low-cost options, these lodgings will make your trip to Oban even more enjoyable.

Selecting The Suitable Accommodation

Choosing the ideal hotel for your visit in Oban is critical to having a comfortable and happy experience. With so many alternatives available, it's critical to consider your interests, budget, and travel style when deciding where to stay.

Here are some aspects to consider while selecting the best lodging for you:

Location: Consider the location of your hotel in proximity to the sights and activities you want to do in Oban. Whether you choose a waterfront hotel with panoramic views or a private getaway in the countryside, select a location that complements your itinerary and provides easy access to the attractions and amenities you seek.

Amenities: Take note of the accommodation's amenities, such as onsite eating, recreational facilities, and complimentary services. Decide which amenities are crucial for your visit, such as a fitness center, free Wi-Fi, or a full Scottish breakfast, and select accommodations that fulfill your requirements.

Budget: Set a budget for your accommodations and stick to it. Oban has accommodation alternatives to suit every budget, from luxurious resorts to low-cost guesthouses and hostels. Consider your budget and look for accommodations that provide the most value for money.

Reviews And Ratings: Read previous guests' reviews and ratings to get a sense of the general quality and experience of the hotel. Look for accommodations with excellent feedback and high ratings for cleanliness, comfort, and customer service. Take note of any common themes or difficulties highlighted in the reviews that may impact your visit.

Accessibility: If you have specific accessibility needs or mobility concerns, please sure to ask about wheelchair ramps, elevators, and accessible rooms when reserving your stay. Choose lodging that meets your requirements and ensures a comfortable stay.

Special Offers And Packages: Keep an eye out for any special offers, deals, or packages that may be available for your preferred accommodation. Many hotels and guesthouses provide discounts for reserving in advance, spending multiple nights, or visiting during off-peak seasons. Take advantage of these promotions to save money on your stay.

Own Tastes: When selecting lodging, consider your own tastes and travel style. Whether you choose a cozy bed and breakfast with a homey ambiance or a modern hotel with sleek design and services, find lodging that suits your needs and enriches your whole experience in Oban.

Booking Tips And Tricks

Booking accommodation in Oban can be simple if you follow these tips and strategies to locate the greatest offers and ensure a smooth booking process:

Book In Advance: To ensure the greatest pricing and availability, book your Oban accommodation well in advance, particularly during busy tourist seasons and major events. Early booking also gives you more options and freedom when selecting the ideal place to stay.

Compare Rates: Use online booking platforms and comparison websites to compare the rates and features provided by various Oban lodgings. Use filters and sorting tools to narrow down your search and locate the greatest bargains that fit your needs.

Look For Specials: Keep an eye out for any specials, discounts, or special offers that may be available for your preferred accommodations. Check the hotel's official website, social media outlets, and third-party booking platforms for special offers and packages.

Consider Flexible Dates: If your trip dates are flexible, you can change your schedule to take advantage of reduced rates and better bargains. Off-peak seasons and midweek stays are typically more economical, so be flexible with your travel plans to save money on lodging.

Read The Fine Print: Before reserving accommodations, thoroughly review the terms and conditions, cancellation policies, and any additional fees or penalties that may be applicable. Pay attention to the booking information and make sure you understand the policies and processes for adjustments or cancellations.

Contact The Accommodation Directly: If you have unique demands or preferences, you should contact the accommodation directly to discuss your requirements and inquire about any special arrangements. This can help ensure that your expectations are met and that any specific needs are accommodated throughout your visit.

Join Loyalty Programs: Hotels and booking platforms offer loyalty programs and membership clubs that allow you to earn points, rewards, and unique privileges with each booking. Take advantage of member-only discounts, upgrades, and benefits to improve your stay and save money on future bookings.

By following these booking tips and tactics, you can locate the ideal accommodation in Oban that suits your needs, tastes, and budget, assuring a memorable and comfortable stay in this picturesque seaside town.

CHAPTER 4

OUTDOOR ACTIVITIES IN OBAN

Oban, located on Scotland's west coast, is an outdoor enthusiast's heaven. This gorgeous coastal town offers plenty of adventure, from exploring rough coasts to journeying into the heart of the Scottish Highlands.

In this chapter, we'll look at some of Oban's most exciting outdoor activities, such as cruises to the Isles, hiking trails, sea kayaking, and animal watching.

Cruise To The Isles

Take a sail to the adjacent islands surrounding Oban for an amazing experience. Even if you're looking for breathtaking scenery, ancient ruins, or lively wildlife, these island cruises provide a one-of-a-kind opportunity to discover the natural beauty and rich history of Scotland's western islands. The following are some popular island cruise destinations from Oban:

Isle Of Mull: Take a cruise to the Isle of Mull and explore its different landscapes, which range from rough coasts and sandy beaches to towering mountains and calm lochs. Explore the vibrant town of Tobermory, see historic castles and old ruins, and keep a look out for wildlife including eagles, otters, and seals.

Staffa And Fingal's Cave: Visit the isolated island of Staffa and marvel at the bizarre geological wonders, which include the well-known Fingal's Cave. Take a guided tour of the island, wander along the rough coastline, and listen for the haunting echoes of the cave's unique acoustics.

Iona: Discover the hallowed island of Iona, including its historic abbey, burial grounds, and stunning beaches. Learn about the island's religious significance and connections to early Christianity, then take a leisurely stroll around the tranquil scenery.

The Treshnish Isles: Set sail for the secluded Treshnish Isles and explore their stunning cliffs, sea caves, and diverse birds. Look for puffins, guillemots, and razorbills nesting on the cliffs, and enjoy the stunning views of the surrounding seascape.

Oban Bay Wildlife Cruises: Take a wildlife cruise around Oban Bay and the surrounding waterways to see seals, dolphins, and porpoises frolic in their natural habitat. Learn about the marine life and ecology of the area from professional guides while taking in the stunning views from the boat.

Hiking Trails

Oban and its surroundings provide a wealth of hiking routes suitable for all levels of experience and fitness. Every outdoor enthusiast can find a trail to enjoy, from simple beach walks to difficult mountain excursions. Lace up your hiking boots and experience Oban's natural beauty by foot with these excellent hiking trails:

Oban Bay Path: Take a leisurely stroll down the Oban Bay Path to enjoy panoramic views of the town's harbor, islands, and surrounding hills. This short coastal walk takes you from Oban town center to Ganavan Sands, passing through gorgeous beaches, forests, and vistas along the route.

Dunollie Woodland Walk: Take a picturesque walk through the historic woodlands of Dunollie Estate, which overlooks Oban Bay. Explore the serene forests, meadows, and gardens, as well as ancient sites like Dunollie Castle and the remnants of St. Columba's Chapel.

Ben Lora Trail: Take a trek up Ben Lora, a famous hill that overlooks Oban. The Ben Lora Trail is a somewhat difficult climb through woodlands and moorland to the peak, where you will be rewarded with panoramic views of Oban, the surrounding islands, and the Mull Mountains.

Ganavan Sands Coastal Walk: Take the coastal walk from Ganavan Sands to Dunstaffnage Castle for spectacular views of the Firth of Lorn and the Isle of Kerrera. This easy-to-moderate walk takes you past sandy beaches, rocky coasts, and grassy headlands, with lots of opportunity to view birds and wildlife along the route.

Isle Of Kerrera Circular stroll: Take a short ferry ride from Oban to the Isle of Kerrera and enjoy a picturesque circular stroll around the island. Hike over steep cliffs, through beautiful fields, and past ancient landmarks such as Gylen Castle and Hutcheson's Monument to take in stunning views of Oban Bay, the Isle of Mull, and the surrounding coast.

Oban has a variety of hiking trails to suit every level of ability and interest, from a leisurely beach walk to a strenuous mountain hike. So, put on your hiking boots, take a picnic, and hit the trails to discover the natural splendor of this breathtaking coastal region.

Sea Kayaking

A sea kayaking experience will allow you to see Oban's magnificent shoreline from a new perspective. Paddle through sheltered beaches, secret coves, and crystal-clear seas to explore the beauty and tranquility of Scotland's west coast.

Half-Day Kayak Tour: Experienced instructors will guide you on a half-day kayak tour of the waterways near Oban. Paddle down the coast, past ancient sites and through gorgeous sea caves, while professional guides teach you about the area's history, animals, and ecology.

Full-Day Kayak Excursion: Set off on a full-day kayak excursion to explore more distant and inaccessible parts of the coastline. Explore adjacent islands, hidden beaches, and secluded bays, with opportunities for wildlife viewing and snorkeling along the route. Stop for a picnic lunch on a remote beach and enjoy the breathtaking views.

Sunset Kayak Tour: A guided kayak tour allows you to see the magic of Oban's coastline at sunset. Paddle out into the calm waters of the bay as the sun sets behind the mountains, sending a golden glow across the landscape. Watch the sky change colors and listen to nature's noises as you glide through the water.

Multi-Day Kayaking Journey: For the ultimate sea kayaking experience, embark on a multi-day journey around Scotland's west coast. Explore lonely islands, craggy coasts, and hidden sea lochs, and sleep under the stars on desolate beaches. Immerse yourself in the environment and enjoy the freedom of sea kayaking in one of Scotland's most scenic and secluded areas.

Sea kayaking in Oban is a unique opportunity to see the Scottish coast's pristine waters, plentiful wildlife, and breathtaking landscape.

Wildlife Watching

Oban and its surrounding waterways are alive with wildlife, making it an ideal destination for environment lovers and wildlife watchers.

This coastal location is home to a diverse range of animals, including majestic marine creatures and secretive seabirds.

Join a guided wildlife trip or go on your own expedition to see some of Scotland's most iconic and fascinating animals.

Here are some wildlife-watching activities to enjoy in Oban:

Whale And Dolphin Watching: Take a boat tour from Oban and explore the vast waters of the Inner Hebrides in search of whales and dolphins. Keep an eye out for minke whales, porpoises, and bottlenose dolphins frolicking in the waves, and learn about their habits and conservation from expert guides.

Seabird Spotting: Puffins, guillemots, and razorbills can all be found breeding on coastal cliffs and rocky outcrops in Oban. Take a boat ride to islands like Lunga and Staffa to get close to these seabird colonies and view them in their natural environment.

Seal Watching: Oban Bay and its surrounding seas are home to a resident population of harbor seals, who can be seen lounging on rocky shores or bobbing in the sea. Join a guided boat tour or rent a kayak and paddle out to seal colonies to see these playful creatures in their natural environment.

Birdwatching: Explore Oban's different habitats, which range from woodlands and wetlands to coastal cliffs and moorlands, and spot a variety of bird species.

Keep a watch out for raptors like golden eagles and buzzards flying overhead, as well as waders, waterfowl, and songbirds in their native habitats.

Red Deer Safaris: Join a guided red deer safari across the Scottish Highlands to see one of Britain's most iconic native species.

Learn about red deer behavior and ecology as you explore their natural habitat, with opportunities for wildlife photography and observation.

Oban's rich and diversified ecosystem provides numerous possibilities for animal viewing and nature appreciation.

With a little patience and luck, you're sure to have some spectacular wildlife encounters during your stay in Oban.

CHAPTER 5

DINING AND CULINARY EXPERIENCES

Oban, dubbed the "Seafood Capital of Scotland," has a delightful selection of eating alternatives and culinary experiences that highlight the region's rich gastronomic legacy. Oban's eating scene will tempt your taste buds with fresh seafood collected daily in the surrounding waters, as well as hearty Scottish fare and artisanal delights.

In this chapter, we'll look at some of Oban's top dining options and culinary experiences, such as seafood restaurants, traditional Scottish fare, cafés and bakeries, and whisky tastings.

Seafood Restaurants

Oban, a seaside town on the Atlantic Ocean, is well-known for its quantity of fresh seafood, which is prominently featured on the menus of its numerous eateries. Oban has an abundance of delectable seafood dishes to choose from, including succulent langoustines and plump scallops, tender salmon, and flaky haddock.

Here are some of the best seafood restaurants to enjoy the flavors of the sea:

Ee-Usk: Located on the waterfront and facing Oban Bay, Ee-usk is a seafood lover's dream. This award-winning restaurant serves a variety of delectable dishes, including classic fish & chips, inventive seafood platters, and shellfish delicacies, all of which are locally sourced and sustainably caught. Don't pass up the opportunity to dine al fresco on the restaurant's outside patio, where you can enjoy panoramic views of the bay while indulging in delicious seafood delights.

Cuan Mor: Located in the heart of Oban's town center, Cuan Mor is a contemporary seafood restaurant and alehouse that showcases the best of Scottish cuisine and hospitality. This popular cafe caters to everyone with a broad menu of seafood classics and modern adaptations, as well as a selection of craft beers and whiskies. Try the local oysters, a seafood soup, or the catch of the day cooked to perfection by the restaurant's outstanding chefs.

Coast: Located in the charming village of Benderloch, only a short drive from Oban, Coast is a hidden gem noted for its delicious seafood and breathtaking views of the surrounding coastline. The restaurant's menu, which focuses on seasonal and locally sourced ingredients, features the best of Scotland's larder, from hand-dived scallops and West Coast mussels to pan-seared sea bass and grilled lobster. Dine in the restaurant's magnificent dining room or on the outside patio and enjoy the peaceful atmosphere and friendly service.

Waterfront Fishouse Restaurant: Perched on the edge of Oban's North Pier, overlooking the bustling harbor, the Waterfront Fishouse Restaurant provides a one-of-a-kind dining experience with breathtaking views of the sea. Enjoy a variety of freshly caught seafood, including West Coast oysters, langoustines, and Loch Fyne salmon, masterfully prepared by the restaurant's talented chefs. Pair your meal with a glass of wine or a dram of whisky from the vast drinks menu, then toast to the flavors of the sea.

Traditional Scottish Fare

In addition to seafood, Oban has a range of restaurants and diners that provide traditional Scottish dishes, highlighting the Highlands and Islands' rich culinary traditions. From robust stews to savory pies to delicate pastries and sweet desserts, there's something for every taste.

Here are some popular venues to eat traditional Scottish cuisine in Oban:

The Olive Garden: Located on a picturesque cobblestone lane in Oban's town center, The Olive Garden is a quiet café noted for its friendly welcome and delicious Scottish cuisine. Feast on hearty meals like haggis neeps and tatties, Scotch broth, and venison stew, all created with locally sourced ingredients and presented with plenty of Scottish warmth. Save room for dessert, and finish your meal with a classic cranachan or sticky toffee pudding.

The Seafood Temple: Located on the outskirts of Oban and facing the picturesque Sound of Kerrera, The Seafood Temple is a hidden gem that serves classic Scottish seafood dishes with a modern twist. Sample delights like smoked haddock and potato soup, Cullen skink, and Argyll lamb, all presented with a variety of seasonal vegetables and locally sourced ingredients. Pair your meal with a bottle of wine or a pint of ale from the restaurant's large drinks menu and take in the tranquil atmosphere and breathtaking views.

Piazza: Located in the heart of Oban's town center, Piazza is a family-friendly restaurant and café that serves classic Scottish and international cuisine. From traditional haggis, neeps, and tatties to hearty steak and ale pie, the menu has something for everyone. The restaurant also serves a variety of freshly made cakes and pastries, ideal for enjoying a sweet treat with your tea or coffee.

The Oban Inn: Built in the 18th century, The Oban Inn is a historic tavern and restaurant in Oban's town center. With its quiet setting, historic décor, and friendly personnel, it's the ideal spot to sample Scotland's culinary heritage. Feast on traditional meals like stovies, bangers and mash, and fisherman's pie, washed down with a pint of locally produced ale or a dram of whisky from the wide drinks menu.

Cafes And Bakeries

Oban boasts a charming collection of cafés and bakeries where you can have freshly brewed coffee, delectable pastries, and handcrafted delicacies.

Here are some of the best cafés and bakeries to visit in Oban:

Oban Chocolate Company: Indulge in a luscious chocolatey delight at Oban Chocolate Company, nestled in the heart of Oban's town center. This artisanal chocolate shop and café serves a delectable selection of handcrafted chocolates, truffles, and confections, as well as freshly brewed coffee and hot chocolate made with real Scottish milk. Indulge in a slice of chocolate cake or a variety of chocolates to go.

The Little Potting Shed Café: Escape the hustle and bustle of Oban's town center and head to The Little Potting Shed Café, which is set in the calm surroundings of Oban's Rockfield Centre. This quaint café, housed in a charming garden shed, has a relaxing environment and serves handcrafted cakes, pastries, and light nibbles. It's the ideal place to have a leisurely breakfast or lunch while surrounded by nature. Sip a freshly brewed cup of coffee or tea and enjoy a slice of freshly baked cake or a warm scone with jam and cream while taking in the tranquil atmosphere.

Oban Bay Coffee Company: Start your day off well with a visit to Oban Bay Coffee Company, a popular café and roastery on Oban's North Pier. Enjoy the rich aroma of freshly roasted coffee beans while sipping on a cup of carefully brewed coffee produced from locally sourced beans. Pair your coffee with a freshly baked croissant or breakfast sandwich cooked with locally sourced ingredients, and take in panoramic views of the harbor and neighboring islands from the café's riverfront setting.

Nories Café: Take a step back in time at Nories Café, a quaint retro-style café in Oban's town center. With its classic décor, nostalgic environment, and friendly service, it's the ideal spot to experience traditional Scottish hospitality. Enjoy a full breakfast, homemade soup, or traditional afternoon tea, all served on old china and complemented by a variety of homemade cakes and pastries.

Bakery Cafe: Located on a side street in Oban's town center, Bakery Cafe is a hidden gem famed for its delectable baked bread, pastries, and cakes. Come in for a freshly baked loaf of bread, a variety of sweet and savory pastries, or a slice of cake created with locally sourced ingredients. Sit at one of the café's comfortable tables or take your sweets to go and eat them while exploring Oban's streets.

Whisky Tasting

No trip to Scotland would be complete without trying the country's most famous commodity, whisky.

Oban, located in the heart of Scotland's whisky-producing region, provides numerous opportunities to sample and learn about this renowned beverage.

Oban Distillery: Take a guided tour of the distillery and learn about the process of producing this well-known single malt whisky.

Discover the distillation process, from malting and mashing to fermentation and maturation, as you tour the ancient distillery and its traditional copper pot stills. Finish your tour with a guided tasting of Oban's iconic whiskies, including the classic Oban 14-Year-Old, to obtain a better understanding of the complexity and flavor of Scotch whisky.

Whiskey Bars: Oban has several whiskey bars where you may try a variety of Scotch whiskies from distilleries throughout Scotland.

Pull yourself a stool at the Oban Inn or The Lorne Bar and study their vast whisky menus, which include a wide range of single malts, blends, and uncommon bottlings. Chat with skilled bartenders and fellow whisky fans while sipping drams of your favorite whiskies and discovering new ones along the way.

Whisky Tasting Experiences: Take a whisky tasting tour led by a professional whisky specialist and travel through Scotland's whisky districts without leaving Oban. Sample whiskies from various distilleries, each highlighting the distinct flavors and characteristics of its area, and learn about its history, production, and tasting notes. Whether you favor peaty Islay malts, fruity Speyside whiskies, or strong Highland drams, there's a tasting experience to fit your tastes.

Whiskey Festivals And Events: Keep a look out for whiskey festivals and events held in and around Oban throughout the year. From whisky tastings and masterclasses to distillery tours and special releases, these events provide a unique opportunity to immerse yourself in the world of Scotch whisky while also connecting with other whisky fans. Sample rare and limited-edition whiskies, meet the people behind the companies, and learn about the art and craft of whisky manufacturing in Scotland.

Whatever whiskey tasting experience you choose, you will undoubtedly obtain a better understanding of Scotland's national drink, as well as the rich legacy and tradition that surround it.

So, raise a glass, appreciate the flavors, and toast to the spirit of Scotland amid Oban's thriving whiskey scene.

CHAPTER 6

SHOPPING IN OBAN

Oban provides a great shopping experience, with a broad choice of stores catering to all tastes and preferences.

This chapter will look at the best locations to shop in Oban, including souvenir shops, local markets, craft boutiques, and specialist stores.

Souvenir Shops

If you want to take home a piece of Oban's charm, souvenir shops are the best location to find mementos and keepsakes to commemorate your visit. These businesses sell everything from traditional Scottish tartan to unusual presents and novelty things, so there's something for everyone.

Here are some popular souvenir shops to visit in Oban:

Oban Whisky And Fine Wines Shop: Located in the heart of Oban's town center, this shop offers a diverse assortment of whiskies, wines, and spirits, ideal for bringing a taste of Scotland home with you. Browse their selection of superb Scottish whiskies, which includes single malts, blends, and limited-edition releases, and purchase a bottle to share with friends and family or as a special gift for a whisky enthusiast.

Oban Chocolate Company: Treat yourself to a delectable souvenir from the Oban Chocolate Company, which offers a tempting selection of handmade chocolates, truffles, and confections. Indulge in a box of gourmet chocolates produced with locally sourced ingredients, or select a variety of delicious treats to enjoy with loved ones at home.

The Tartan Shop: Enter The Tartan Shop and find a treasure trove of Scottish tartan, kilts, and accessories. Browse their collection of traditional tartan patterns and clan crests to find the ideal souvenir to commemorate your trip to Scotland. Whether you are of Scottish origin or simply enjoy the beauty of tartan, this business has something for everyone.

Oban Distillery Gift Store: After your tour of Oban Distillery, stop by the gift store to pick up a bottle of Oban whisky or other whisky-related gifts. From branded glassware and bar accessories to whisky-flavored chocolates and fudge, you'll find a variety of unique presents to commemorate your distillery visit.

Local Markets

Visit one of Oban's lively markets for a taste of local flavor as well as an opportunity to mix with the locals. These markets provide a colorful shopping experience unlike any other, featuring fresh produce and specialty delicacies, as well as handmade crafts and unusual gifts.

Here are several must-see marketplaces in Oban:

Oban Farmer's Market: The Oban Farmer's Market is held on select occasions throughout the year and features the best of Argyll's local produce, artisanal delicacies, and handmade crafts. Stroll through the market stalls and sample a wide range of products, including fresh fruits and vegetables, artisan cheeses, handcrafted jams and preserves, baked goodies, and more. Chat with the friendly merchants to learn about the tales behind their products, and pick up some tasty sweets to enjoy while in Oban or to take home as gifts.

Oban Indoor Market: Situated in the heart of Oban's town center, the Oban Indoor Market is a hive of activity, with traders offering everything from apparel and jewelry to artwork and antiques. Browse the stalls to find a wide variety of items, including handmade crafts, vintage treasures, and one-of-a-kind souvenirs.

Oban Artisan Market: Held monthly in the picturesque settings of Station Square, the Oban Artisan Market is a must-see for fans of handmade crafts and artisanal goods. Browse the stalls and enjoy the work of local artisans, who display their skills in a range of mediums such as pottery, textiles, woodworking, and more. This colorful market has something for everyone, from one-of-a-kind home decor products to handcrafted jewelry and accessories.

Craft Boutiques

Oban's artisan boutiques are an excellent place to find handmade gifts and locally manufactured things. These quaint boutiques highlight the abilities of local craftsmen and provide a carefully curated collection of handmade gifts, home decor items, and wearable art.

Here are several craft boutiques to visit in Oban:

Sea Tangle Studio: Located in Oban's town center, Sea Tangle Studio is a paradise for those who enjoy handmade goods and coastal-inspired decor. Browse their range of handcrafted ceramics, textiles, and artwork inspired by the natural beauty of Scotland's coastline. Each creation, from sea glass jewelry and driftwood sculptures to hand-painted pottery and screen-printed fabrics, reflects Oban's maritime past in its own distinctive way.

Sorcha Crafts: Located in a historic building overlooking Oban Bay, Sorcha Crafts is a family-owned business that specializes in handmade gifts and Scottish souvenirs. Step inside to browse their collection of locally manufactured products, such as knitwear, pottery, artwork, and more. Sorcha Crafts has everything you're looking for, whether it's a comfortable wool sweater, gorgeous ceramics, or a one-of-a-kind piece of artwork to hang on your walls.

Tweed And Tartan: Tweed and Tartan is a boutique dedicated to Scotland's renowned fabrics. Browse their selection of tweed jackets, kilts, scarves, and accessories, all produced from the best Scottish wool and created by expert artisans.

Specialty Stores

Oban has a number of specialty boutiques that provide one-of-a-kind items and gourmet foods that cannot be found elsewhere.

These specialty boutiques cater to discerning shoppers looking for something unique, offering artisanal delicacies, fine wines, handmade crafts, and luxury goods. Here are some specialty shops to visit in Oban:

Green Room: Treat your senses at The Green Room, a specialist food store and deli in Oban's town center. Stock up on gourmet items like locally smoked salmon, artisan cheeses, handmade chocolates, and gourmet condiments, which are ideal for preparing a picnic or gourmet meal at home. Before you go, try some of the store's delightful delicacies and pick up a bottle of wine or whisky to pair with your supper.

Oban Fine Wines: Oban Fine Wines is a haven for oenophiles and wine fans, offering fine wines, spirits, and liqueurs from all over the world. Browse their expertly curated variety of wines, champagnes, and whiskies, and let their educated staff help you discover the ideal bottle for any occasion. Oban Fine Wines has it; and it doesn't if you want a particular vintage to commemorate a milestone or a one-of-a-kind present for a wine enthusiast.

The Tartan Company: Enter The Tartan Company to explore a world of Scottish luxury and heritage. This business specializes in tartan clothes, accessories, and presents, and it offers a carefully curated collection of high-quality goods manufactured from the best wool and textiles. Browse their selection of tartan scarves, shawls, ties, and kilts, all made by professional artisans using traditional methods.

The Chocolate Box: Give yourself a taste of luxury at The Chocolate Box, a specialty boutique that sells handcrafted chocolates and confections prepared with the best ingredients. Indulge in a variety of artisanal chocolates, truffles, and pralines, all painstakingly made by professional chocolatiers. From conventional milk chocolate bars to exotic fruit-filled truffles, The Chocolate Box has something to fulfill every craving.

Oban Art Gallery: Immerse yourself in Oban's thriving arts scene by visiting the Oban Art Gallery, a boutique that showcases the work of local artists and artisans. Explore their collection of paintings, sculptures, pottery, and fabrics, admiring the variety of styles and techniques on show. Oban

Art Gallery has something to inspire everyone, whether they are seasoned art collectors or simply admire excellent craftsmanship.

Oban's specialized businesses provide a one-of-a-kind shopping experience that highlights the best of Scottish craftsmanship and creativity, with everything from souvenirs and local crafts to gourmet cuisine and luxury items.

So, take your time, explore the stores, and find things to take home from your vacation to this little coastal town.

CHAPTER 7

DAY TRIPS FROM OBAN

Oban is a good starting point for exploring the beautiful scenery, historic attractions, and picturesque communities that surround it.

From rocky coasts and majestic mountains to old castles and picturesque lochs, there are plenty of opportunities for adventure just outside of town.

In this chapter, we'll look at some of the best day trips from Oban, each with their own distinct blend of natural beauty, cultural legacy, and outdoor activities.

Island Of Mull

The Isle of Mull, only a short ferry ride from Oban, is a nature lover's and outdoor enthusiast's dream. Mull's rocky coastline, rolling hills, and diverse fauna provide limitless options for exploration and adventure.

Here are some highlights from a day trip to the Isle of Mull:

Tobermory: Begin your day excursion by experiencing the vibrant town of Tobermory, which is noted for its brilliantly painted buildings, picturesque port, and lively waterfront. Take a stroll down the waterfront promenade, peruse the stores and galleries, and stop by the Tobermory Distillery to enjoy some of the island's best whisky.

Mull Eagle Watch: Take a guided eagle-watching excursion with Mull Eagle Watch to see one of Mull's most iconic residents. Accompanied by skilled guides, explore the island's rugged and desolate landscapes in search of golden and white-tailed eagles, as well as other natural animals including red deer, otters and seals.

Fingal's Cave: Take in the natural beauty of Fingal's Cave, a sea cave located on the deserted island of Staffa, off the coast of Mull. The cave, built from hexagonal basalt columns and flanked by stunning cliffs, is a sight to behold and may be reached by boat from Mull's shores.

Duart Castle: Take a step back in time and see Duart Castle, an enormous fortification built on a cliff overlooking the Sound of Mull. Explore the castle's medieval rooms, take in the breathtaking views from the battlements, and learn about the Maclean clan, who have called Duart Castle home for generations.

Isle Of Staffa

Staffa is a small, deserted island near the Isle of Mull famed for its magnificent basalt columns and sea caves. Staffa boasts some of Scotland's most magnificent natural beauty.

What to See and Do on a Day Trip to the Isle of Staffa:

Fingal's Cave: The highlight of any trip to Staffa is Fingal's Cave, a breathtaking sea cave known for its hexagonal basalt columns and strange acoustics. Take a boat to the island and disembark at the landing stage, where you may walk through the cave and admire its unearthly splendor.

Animals Watching: Keep a look out for animals on your cruise to Staffa, since the waterways surrounding the island are alive with marine life. Look for puffins, guillemots, and razorbills nesting on the cliffs, seals sunning on the rocks, and dolphins playing in the waters.

Am Buachaille: If you're feeling daring, attempt ascending to the summit of Am Buachaille, Staffa's highest point. From the top, you'll be rewarded with panoramic views of the surrounding sea and shoreline, as well as awe of the island's rugged beauty.

Glencoe

As you travel inland from Oban, you will come upon Glencoe, one of Scotland's most iconic and spectacular landscapes. Glencoe, located in the Scottish Highlands, is known for its towering mountains, deep glens, and stormy past.

Here's what to see during a day trip to Glencoe:

Hiking: Lace up your boots and hit the trails to explore Glencoe by foot. Choose from a selection of hiking paths suitable for all ability levels, from pleasant strolls along glen floors to strenuous climbs up steep peaks. Popular hikes include Lost Valley, Devil's Staircase, and Buachaille Etive Mor.

Visitor Center: Learn about Glencoe's history, geology, and animals at the Glencoe Visitor Center, which is nestled in the middle of the glen. Browse interactive exhibits, watch interesting movies, and speak with expert personnel who may offer ideas and information on visiting the area.

Photography: Glencoe is a photographer's heaven, with its spectacular scenery and ever-changing light. Bring your camera and capture the grandeur of the glen at sunrise or sunset, when the mountains are illuminated by golden light and the surrounding scenery is at its most evocative.

Inveraray

Inveraray, located on the beaches of Loch Fyne, is a lovely town recognized for its medieval architecture, natural beauty, and rich cultural legacy. A day trip to Inveraray allows you to visit historic sites, participate in outdoor activities, and learn about traditional Scottish culture. What to See and Do in Inveraray:

Inveraray Castle: Discover the spectacular gardens and interiors of Inveraray Castle, the Duke of Argyll's ancestral residence. Wander through the castle's sumptuous rooms and wonderfully planted gardens, admiring the grand architecture, lavish furniture, and remarkable art collection.

Inveraray Jail: Take a step back in time by visiting Inveraray Jail, a living museum that provides an intriguing peek into Scotland's penal history. Explore the historic courtroom, jail cells, and exhibits that depict the life of prisoners and personnel in the nineteenth century.

Loch Fyne: Take a leisurely stroll around the shores of Loch Fyne to enjoy the picturesque beauty of this calm loch. Keep a watch out for wildlife like otters, seals, and seabirds, and take in the spectacular vistas of the surrounding mountains and woodlands.

Shopping And Dining: Explore the shops and galleries in Inveraray's lovely town center, where you can find a wide range of local crafts, gifts, and souvenirs. After that, unwind in one of the town's charming tearooms or traditional pubs, where you can savor delectable Scottish cuisine and local fish.

From island adventures to mountain hikes and historic locations, Oban day tours provide a wide choice of experiences that highlight Scotland's natural beauty, cultural legacy, and outdoor activities.

It doesn't matter if you're exploring the rugged coastline of Mull, marveling at the geological wonders of Staffa, trekking in the gorgeous mountains of Glencoe, or immersing yourself in the history and charm of Inveraray, each site promises an unforgettable day of discovery and exploration.

CHAPTER 8

FESTIVALS AND EVENTS IN OBAN

Oban is famed for its breathtaking vistas and rich history, as well as its active cultural scene and year-round festivals and events. From traditional Highland sports to music festivals and agricultural exhibitions, there is always something spectacular going on in this coastal town.

In this chapter, we'll look at some of Oban's most popular festivals and events, each of which provides a unique insight into the local culture and heritage.

Oban Winter Festival

The Oban Winter Festival kicks off the holiday season in style, celebrating everything winter with a jam-packed calendar of events and activities for guests of all ages. From traditional markets and craft fairs to live music performances and seasonal entertainment, there's a lot to see and do at this magical time of year.

Here is what to expect during the Oban Winter Festival.

Christmas Market: Browse the stalls at the Oban Christmas Market to find one-of-a-kind gifts, handmade crafts, and seasonal delights from local artisans and sellers. From hand-knitted sweaters and woolen scarves to homemade preserves and gourmet chocolates, you'll discover a diverse selection of items to complete your holiday buying list.

Street Food Festival: Treat your taste buds to the Oban Street Food Festival, where you may sample delectable cuisine from all over the world, created by local chefs and food merchants. From gourmet burgers and wood-fired pizzas to authentic Thai cuisine and freshly shucked oysters, this culinary extravaganza caters to every craving.

Live Music Performances: Local bands and artists perform live at various venues in Oban, including pubs, bars, and outdoor stages. From traditional Scottish folk music to current pop and rock, the festival lineup caters to a wide range of musical preferences.

Community Events: Join in the holiday spirit with a variety of community events and activities, such as carol singing, tree lighting ceremonies, and Santa's grotto visits. Bring the whole family and get into the festive spirit by exploring Oban's lovely streets, which are decked with dazzling lights and decorations.

Highland Games

The Highland Games have been a beloved Scottish event for generations, highlighting the country's rich cultural legacy and sporting ability.

The Highland Games, held yearly in towns and villages throughout Scotland, including Oban, are a display of strength, skill, and solidarity, with athletes competing in traditional Scottish sports such as caber tossing, hammer throwing, and tug-of-war.

Here is what to expect during the Oban Highland Games.

Athletic Competitions: Watch athletes from all around Scotland and beyond compete in classic Highland sports such as the caber toss, stone put, weight throw, and hammer throw. Marvel at the participants' strength and ability as they compete for honors in these ancient contests of strength and endurance.

Pipe Band Performances: Listen to the rousing sound of the bagpipes as pipe bands from across the region compete in spirited musical performances. Listen to the haunting melodies and powerful drumbeats as the bands march and perform, adding to the celebratory atmosphere of the games.

Traditional Dancing: Be charmed by traditional Scottish dancers who perform complicated choreography and spirited reels to the accompaniment of fiddles and accordions. Join in the fun by trying your hand (or feet) at some Highland dancing, or simply sitting back and admiring the spectacle.

Craft Booths And Food Sellers: Explore the craft booths and food sellers that line the games field for a selection of handmade crafts, artisanal products, and delectable delicacies. The Highland Games provide something for everyone, from tartan kilts and handcrafted jewelry to freshly baked pies and hearty stews.

Oban Live Music Festival

Music lovers, rejoice! The Oban Live Music Festival is a highlight of the town's cultural calendar, featuring the best Scottish and international music talent through a series of spectacular performances and concerts. From folk and rock to jazz and blues, the festival has something for everyone's musical taste.

Here's what to expect at Oban Live:

Headline Bands: Prepare to rock out with some of the biggest names in music as headline bands take the stage to electrify the crowds. The program, which includes chart-topping bands and iconic solo artists, is sure to captivate music aficionados of all ages.

Local Talent: Discover Scotland's richness of musical talent as local bands and artists perform on stage. From up-and-coming indie bands to seasoned folk musicians, the event allows budding artists to share their music with a larger audience.

Outdoor Concerts: Experience the festival atmosphere with outdoor concerts and shows in various spots throughout

Oban. Dance the night away under the stars while listening to live music amidst the town's lovely shoreline and breathtaking natural surroundings.

Late-Night Sessions: Keep the party going with late-night and jam sessions in Oban's pubs and bars. Join in the excitement as musicians meet to perform impromptu sets and spontaneous collaborations, resulting in a dynamic atmosphere that should not be missed.

Highland Cattle Show

The Highland Cattle Show in Oban offers a taste of rural Scotland as well as the opportunity to observe some of the country's most renowned livestock up close. This annual agricultural festival honors the Highland breed of cattle, which is recognized for its unusual shaggy coats, majestic horns, and mild demeanor.

Here's things to see and do during the Highland Cattle Show:

Cattle Judging: Watch breeders show off their prized Highland cattle in a variety of competitions and judging events. Admire the beauty and majesty of these amazing animals as they parade about the show ring, competing for top prizes in categories such as best bull, best cow, and best young handler.

Livestock Displays: In addition to Highland cattle, the exhibition showcases sheep, goats, and pigs. As you roam through the pens and paddocks, marvel at the richness of Scotland's agricultural past while learning about the many breeds and their unique traits.

Crafts And Produce: Visit the Highland Cattle Show's craft stalls and food sellers to find a wide range of handmade goods, artisanal products, and locally sourced foods and beverages. From hand-knitted sweaters and fuzzy socks to homemade jams and preserves, the fair has something for everyone.

Educational Demonstrations: Throughout the day, there will be a variety of educational demonstrations and workshops where you can learn about traditional farming practices and Scottish rural living. Watch professional craftsmen practice processes like sheep shearing, wool spinning, and blacksmithing to learn about the skills and traditions that have created Scotland's agricultural legacy.

Oban's festivals and events, which range from festive festivities and cultural events to agricultural shows and music festivals, cater to everyone.

CHAPTER 9

FAMILY-FRIENDLY ACTIVITIES

Oban isn't just for adults; it's also a great spot for families to do a variety of things together. There's something for everyone in the family, from seeing marine life to enjoying sweet sweets and going on outdoor activities.

In this chapter, we'll look at some of the best family-friendly activities in Oban that are sure to make unforgettable experiences for everyone.

Sea Life Sanctuary

The Scottish SEA LIFE Sanctuary in Oban offers an instructive and fascinating day out for the whole family. This marine conservation center is home to a wide range of intriguing aquatic species, including playful seals and mischievous otters, as well as bright fish and mesmerizing jellyfish.

Here's what to expect at the Sealife Sanctuary:

Interactive Displays: Explore the aquarium's interactive displays to learn about the various marine species that lives in Scotland's coastal waters. From touch pools where you can get up close to starfish and crabs to underwater tunnels where you can see sharks and rays move overhead, there's something for everyone.

Seal Feeding Sessions: Don't miss the daily seal feeding sessions, where you can observe the sanctuary's resident seals being fed by educated staff members. Learn about these amazing creatures and their natural activities, and be amazed with their agility and intellect as they perform tricks and play in the water.

Conservation Talks: Attend interesting conservation talks and presentations given by marine biologists and animal care experts. Discover how the sanctuary is working to safeguard maritime environments and species, and how you can help.

Outdoor Play Area: After viewing the indoor exhibits, let the youngsters burn off some energy in the outdoor play area, which has climbing frames, slides, and other entertaining activities. Relax and enjoy a picnic in the sunshine while the kids run, jump, and play freely.

Paddleboard Lessons

Experience the thrill of paddleboarding with the entire family on Oban Bay's crystal-clear waters. Paddleboarding is a fun and accessible water sport that is appropriate for all ages and skill levels, making it an ideal activity for families wishing to try something new together.

What To Expect From Paddleboarding Classes In Oban:

Teaching And Safety Briefing: Before embarking on your paddleboarding excursion, qualified instructors will provide a safety briefing and teaching session. Learn the fundamentals of paddleboarding techniques, such as how to balance, paddle, and steer your board, as well as important safety guidelines for traversing the water.

Guided Tours: Take a guided paddleboarding tour to see the picturesque shoreline of Oban Bay from a different angle. Paddle past rocky cliffs, hidden coves, and scenic islands, keeping a watch out for animals like seals, seabirds, and even dolphins or porpoises.

Family-Friendly Equipment: Choose from a variety of paddleboards made for multiple riders, such as tandem boards and inflatable SUPs perfect for youngsters. Even the youngest members of the family may participate in the fun and enjoy paddling on the water thanks to competent instructors.

Fun And Games: Make the most of your time on the water with paddleboarding games and activities that the whole family can enjoy. Race each other, play tag, or simply paddle around and explore at your own pace while soaking up the sun and spending valuable time together in the beautiful outdoors.

Oban Chocolate Company

Visit the Oban Chocolate Company to satisfy your sweet craving and treat the entire family to a delectable selection of handcrafted chocolates and confections. From creamy truffles and rich fudge to luscious chocolate bars and whimsical sweets, this famous neighborhood chocolatier has something to fulfill every craving.

Here's what to expect at Oban Chocolate Company:

Chocolate Workshops: Unleash your creativity by learning how to make delectable chocolates from scratch. Mold, dip, and decorate your own chocolates with expert direction, experimenting with different flavors, fillings, and toppers to make one-of-a-kind and personalized delights.

Tasting Sessions: Indulge your taste buds with a chocolate tasting session with a selection of the company's finest chocolates and confections. As you enjoy in a sensory experience unlike any other, you'll learn about the differences in cocoa beans, flavor profiles, and production procedures.

Gift Store: Browse the company's attractive gift store and pick up some delectable delights to take home. Choose from an exciting selection of chocolatey delicacies, all elegantly packed and ready to present to friends and family—or to enjoy as a sweet remembrance of your stay in Oban.

Café: Relax and rest in the company's pleasant café, which serves a variety of enticing treats such as freshly baked pastries, decadent hot chocolates, and creamy milkshakes. Sit back and enjoy your delicious treat while taking in the warm and welcome atmosphere of our family-friendly institution.

Oban Bay Play

Allow the youngsters to burn off some energy and have fun at Oban Bay Play, a family-friendly indoor soft play center located in the heart of Oban. Oban Bay Play's colorful play structures, ball pits, and slides provide hours of amusement for children of all ages, rain or shine.

Here's what to expect at Oban Bay Play:

Soft Play Area: Prepare for a day of fun and adventure in the soft play area, which has a variety of climbing frames, tunnels, and obstacles for children to explore. Watch them crawl, climb, and slide their way around the colorful play structures, honing their motor skills and coordination in the process.

Toddler Zone: The toddler zone is designed with younger children in mind, providing a safe and engaging space for them to play and engage. Let them wild in the ball pit, crawl through the soft tunnels, or ride on the tiny slides, all under the cautious eye of attentive professionals.

Café: Take a break from playtime to recharge at the café, which serves a variety of snacks, drinks, and light meals. Sit back and relax as the kids play, knowing they're having fun in a safe and supervised atmosphere.

Birthday Parties: Celebrate your child's special day at Oban Bay Play, where you will have exclusive access to the play facilities and a designated party area. With personalized party packages that include food, beverages, and entertainment, it's the ideal way to make your child's birthday memorable.

Oban has a variety of family-friendly activities to keep guests of all ages entertained, from exploring marine life and paddleboarding on the bay to indulging in sweet delicacies and burning off energy at the soft play area.

CHAPTER 10

NIGHTLIFE IN OBAN

When the sun sets over Oban's craggy coastline, the town comes alive with a thriving nightlife scene that attracts both locals and visitors.

Oban has a broad range of nightly entertainment options, including historic pubs offering good Scottish beers and lively music venues presenting outstanding artists. Whether you want to relax with a pint by the fire or dance the night away to live music, there is something for everyone to do after dark.

In this chapter, we will look at the greatest pubs, bars, live music venues, whisky bars, and nightclubs Oban has to offer.

Pubs And Bars

Oban has a number of inviting pubs and bars where you can relax, meet new people, and enjoy a wide range of drinks.

From old pubs with crackling fires to modern bars with waterfront views, there's a pub or bar to suit everyone.

Here are some of the greatest pubs and bars to visit in Oban:

The Oban Inn: Located in the heart of town, The Oban Inn is a typical Scottish bar with a comfortable ambiance and a friendly welcome. Pull up a stool at the bar and sip on a pint of locally made ale or one of the pub's superb whiskies while conversing with friendly locals and travelers.

The Waterfront Bar: The Waterfront Bar, located on Oban Bay, provides breathtaking views of the harbor and beyond. Relax on the outdoor terrace with a glass of wine or a cocktail, taking in the atmosphere while you watch the boats arrive and go. Live music performances are a common feature here, contributing to the lively atmosphere.

The Lorne Bar: With its Victorian-era design and delightful character, the Lorne Bar is a popular hangout for both locals and visitors. Step inside and appreciate the magnificent woodwork and stained glass windows while sipping a drink from the well-stocked bar. Try the Lorne Lemonade, the pub's specialty beverage created with locally sourced ingredients and presented with a twist.

The Malt Whisky Bar: Whisky enthusiasts will not want to miss The Malt Whisky Bar, which has one of Oban's largest collections of Scotch whisky. As you sip and relish the flavors of Scotland's national drink, select from a diverse choice of single malts, blends, and unique bottlings. Knowledgeable staff are available to make recommendations and provide instruction for both novice and experienced whisky drinkers.

Live Music Venues

Oban has several of places where talented musicians can perform everything from traditional Scottish folk to current rock and pop. Whether you prefer modest acoustic shows or energetic live bands, there is something for everyone's musical tastes.

Here are some of the best live music venues in Oban:

The View: Located on the Esplanade overlooking Oban Bay, is a famous live music venue with a lively atmosphere and breathtaking views. Sit back with a drink and enjoy acoustic performances by local musicians, or hit the dance floor when the band kicks into high gear.

The Corran Halls: This historic venue hosts a wide range of live music events throughout the year, from classical concerts and jazz performances to rock shows and tribute bands. Check the schedule to see what's going on during your visit, and enjoy the thrill of live music in the heart of Oban.

The Tyree Bar: Tucked away down a side street, The Tyree Bar is a hidden gem famous for its live music and open mic evenings. Join in the excitement as local artists perform on stage, or take a seat at the bar and watch the entertainment while sipping a pint.

The Argyllshire Gathering Halls: This ancient institution hosts regular ceilidh nights featuring Scotland's dynamic rhythms and traditional dances. Join in the excitement as a live band performs traditional tunes and a caller walks you through the steps, creating a joyful atmosphere that will have your feet tapping.

Whisky Bars

No visit to Scotland is complete without drinking some of the country's famous whisky, and Oban has various bars where you can do just that.

Here are some of the best whisky bars in Oban:

Ee-Usk: This waterfront restaurant and bar serves a diverse selection of Scottish whiskies, from well-known brands to rare and limited-edition bottlings. Take a seat at the bar and let the educated staff take you through the selection, discovering new favorites and old classics.

Cuan Mor: Located in a restored church overlooking Oban Bay, Cuan Mor is a sophisticated bar and restaurant with a well-stocked whisky cabinet. Choose from over 100 whiskies from Scottish distilleries, including Oban's own, and enjoy a dram in the exquisite setting of this historic building.

The Oban Whisky And Fine Wines Shop: If you prefer to drink your whisky in the comfort of your own home, stop by The Oban Whisky & Fine Wines Shop, where you may peruse a broad selection of whiskies and other spirits to take home with you. Whether you're searching for a souvenir bottle to remember your trip or a unique gift for a whisky-loving buddy, you'll find lots of alternatives here.

Nightclubs

Oban boasts two nightclubs where you may let loose and party into the early hours. While the town does not have a major club scene like larger cities, these establishments provide a vibrant and active atmosphere for people seeking midnight entertainment.

Here are some of the best nightclubs in Oban:

The Corryvreckan: Named after the famed whirlpool off the coast of Jura, The Corryvreckan nightclub is a popular place for both residents and visitors to dance and socialize. With a DJ spinning the latest hits and a vibrant crowd of partygoers, it's the ideal location to let your hair down and dance till dawn.

The Skipinnish Ceilidh House: For a more traditional Scottish night out, go to The Skipinnish Ceilidh House and enjoy a night of ceilidh dancing and live music. Join in the excitement as a live band performs traditional tunes and a caller walks you through the steps, creating a lively atmosphere that will have everyone on their feet.

Oban has something for everyone as the sun goes down, whether you want a quiet pint in a nice bar, a night of live music and dancing, or an unforgettable whisky tasting experience.

So, get your pals together, hoist a glass, and toast to a wonderful night out in this vibrant coastal town.

CHAPTER 11

WELLNESS AND RELAXATION

Finding moments of tranquility and refreshment is crucial in the bustling town of Oban, where crashing seas meet the craggy coastline.

Chapter 11 delves into the different options for engaging in wellness and relaxation, ranging from opulent spa vacations to exciting outdoor activities.

Spa Retreats

Escape from the stresses of everyday life and immerse yourself in a world of relaxation and pampering at one of Oban's exquisite spa resorts.

From restorative massages to calming facials, these sanctuaries provide a variety of therapies to relieve stress and leave you feeling refreshed and invigorated.

The Spa At Isle Of Eriska Hotel: Located on a secluded island just a short drive from Oban, the Isle of Eriska Hotel has a world-class spa that offers a variety of sensual treatments in stunning natural surroundings. Relax with a hot stone massage, visit the sauna and steam room, or swim in the heated indoor pool, which overlooks the serene waters of Loch Linnhe.

The Lochside Hotel Spa: Located on the beaches of Loch Fyne, the Lochside Hotel Spa is an ideal spot to relax and refresh. Treat yourself to a holistic massage, a detoxifying body wrap, or simply rest in the outdoor hot tub while admiring the tranquil beauty of the Scottish countryside.

The Spa At The Perle Oban Hotel: Located in the heart of Oban, The Perle Oban Hotel provides a relaxing spa experience with a variety of exquisite treatments to select from. From aromatherapy massages to revitalizing facials, each treatment is designed to calm the mind, body, and spirit, leaving you feeling wonderfully relaxed and renewed.

Yoga Studios

Find your inner zen and build a sense of balance and harmony by taking a yoga session at one of Oban's inviting studios.

Oban Yoga: Located in the heart of Oban, Oban Yoga offers a wide range of sessions to suit all levels, from soothing hatha yoga to energetic vinyasa flow. With skilled instructors guiding you through each practice, you'll leave feeling grounded, balanced, and prepared to face whatever life throws at you.

The Studio: Located in a peaceful setting overlooking Oban Bay, The Studio provides a variety of yoga programs aimed at promoting physical, mental, and emotional well-being. Whether you want to increase your flexibility, reduce stress, or simply relax, this pleasant studio has the appropriate session for you.

Yoga By The Sea: As you practice yoga by the sea, listen to the relaxing sound of the waves and enjoy the lovely sea breeze. Yoga by the Sea, situated on the beaches of Loch Linnhe, provides outdoor yoga lessons in a gorgeous natural location, allowing you to connect with nature and achieve inner peace as you flow through your practice.

Outdoor Wellness Activities

Embrace nature's healing power and participate in outdoor wellness activities amidst Oban's stunning landscapes.

Forest Bathing: Immerse yourself in nature's therapeutic power by taking a forest bath in the ancient trees surrounding Oban. Guided by a licensed forest therapy guide, you'll take a soothing sensory trip into the forest, engaging in mindfulness activities and connecting with the natural world in a truly meaningful way.

Meditation By The Loch: Find a quiet area beside one of Oban's stunning lochs and begin your meditation practice amidst the peaceful beauty of the Scottish countryside.

Beach Yoga: Practice yoga on one of Oban's lovely beaches, feeling the sand between your toes and the soothing sea wind against your skin. Beach yoga is a one-of-a-kind opportunity to connect with the elements and find inner calm while listening to the sound of the waves and inhaling salty air.

Wellness Workshops

A wellness class or retreat in Oban can help you expand and deepen your understanding of holistic wellness.

These programs cover everything from mindfulness and meditation to nutrition and self-care, providing essential insights and practical methods for improving your overall well-being and leading a more balanced and fulfilled life.

Mindfulness Retreat: Attend a mindfulness retreat taught by experienced instructors and practitioners to learn how to cultivate present, awareness, and compassion in everyday life. Through guided meditation, mindful movement, and group discussions, you'll learn the fundamentals of mindfulness and build practical methods for stress management and achieving greater peace and contentment.

Nutrition Course: Learn about the power of food as medicine in this nutrition course that focuses on supporting maximum health and vitality through mindful eating and nutritious cuisine. Learn how to make tasty and healthy meals using fresh, seasonal products, as well as practical advice for introducing more plant-based foods into your diet for better energy, digestion, and general health.

Self-Care Getaway: Treat yourself to a self-care getaway that will help you reconnect with yourself and prioritize your health.

From gentle yoga and meditation to decadent spa treatments and creative expression, these retreats provide a comprehensive approach to self-care that nourishes the body, mind, and spirit, leaving you feeling refreshed, restored, and ready to face life with renewed vitality.

In today's fast-paced and chaotic environment, it's more crucial than ever to prioritize our health and well-being.

Oban provides a variety of wellness experiences to help you nourish your body, mind, and soul, whether you're looking for relaxation, renewal, or just a moment of calm in the midst of stress.

So, take a deep breath, slow down, and immerse yourself in the rejuvenating beauty of this little coastal town.

CHAPTER 12

LOCAL ETIQUETTE AND CUSTOMS

To have a seamless and joyful experience while seeing the picturesque town of Oban, you should become acquainted with local etiquette and customs beforehand. Understanding the local social norms and cultural customs will assist you negotiate relationships with locals while also demonstrating respect for their traditions and values.

In this chapter, we'll look at the nuances of Oban etiquette, including greetings and courtesy, as well as tipping standards and eating etiquette.

Greeting And Politeness

In Oban, as in much of Scotland, politeness and friendliness are highly regarded qualities, and greetings are vital in social interactions. When meeting someone for the first time or entering a store or restaurant, a simple "hello" or "good morning" is typically adequate.

Handshakes are customary in official contexts, although a nod or smile is appropriate in more relaxed situations.

When addressing someone, it is traditional to use their title and last name, followed by "Mr." or "Ms." For example, "Mr. Smith" or "Ms. MacLeod." If you are unsure of someone's title, it is advisable to err on the side of formality until you are asked to use their first name.

In social circumstances, it is customary to make eye contact and participate in small conversation, such as commenting on the weather or asking about someone's day. Scots are famed for their friendliness and hospitality, so don't be shocked if strangers approach you in public places.

When leaving, it is usual to say "goodbye" or "cheerio" and express gratitude for the individual's time or assistance.

A warm smile and a nod of the head can also express appreciation and respect.

Tipping Practices

Tipping practices in Oban are comparable to those around the UK, with gratuities not expected but appreciated for exceptional service. In restaurants and bars, it is traditional to leave a tip of 10-15% of the total cost if you have had excellent service.

However, if the bill includes a service charge, additional tipping is unnecessary.

For other services, such as taxi rides or hotel porters, rounding up the fare or leaving a little tip is a courteous way to express gratitude. In hotels, it is common to offer a tip for housekeeping personnel at the conclusion of your stay, usually between £1 and £2 each day.

While tipping is appreciated, it is vital to remember that it should be proportionate to the quality of service provided. If you believe the service was mediocre or unsatisfactory, it is completely appropriate not to give a tip.

Dinner Etiquette

Dining etiquette in Oban is mostly similar to that of the rest of the UK, with a few exceptions. When dining out, it is usual to wait to be seated rather than select a table yourself. Once seated, it is customary to place your napkin on your lap and refrain from beginning your meal until everyone at the table has been served.

In formal eating situations, utensils are used from the outside in, with the fork on the left and the knife on the right. When you're finished eating, place your knife and fork on your plate with the prongs facing up to let the server know you're done.

When sharing a meal, it is courteous to wait until everyone has been served before starting to eat. If someone offers to pass you a meal, it is usual to accept a little quantity rather than a large serving.

At the end of the meal, it is customary to thank the host or server for their hospitality and offer to assist in clearing the table or doing the dishes if dining in someone's house.

Social Norms

Oban, like much of Scotland, has its own set of social standards and practices that tourists should understand in order to interact respectfully with locals. For example, punctuality is highly prized, therefore it is critical to arrive on time for appointments, meetings, and social functions.

Respect for personal space is also vital, so keep a reasonable distance when chatting with people. Interrupting or talking over someone is considered impolite, so wait your turn to speak and listen carefully to what others have to say.

In social situations, it is normal to offer to buy a round of drinks for your party, with each member taking turns covering the expense of one round. This is referred to as "getting a round in" and is a common approach to express hospitality and friendship.

When visiting someone's home, it is customary to offer a little gift, such as a bottle of wine or an arrangement of flowers, to express gratitude for their hospitality. When entering the house, make sure to remove your shoes and respect any other house rules or customs that the host may have.

By being acquainted with local etiquette and customs, you will be better equipped to handle social interactions while also respecting the traditions and values of the Oban community.

It doesn't matter if you're dining out, attending a social occasion, or simply touring the town, a little kindness and consideration will go a long way toward making your time in Oban enjoyable and memorable.

CHAPTER 13

LEARNING BASIC SCOTISH GAELIC

Embracing the language of the country enriches any travel experience by helping you to connect more deeply with the culture and people of a location. Learning basic Scottish Gaelic in Oban, a town with a rich Gaelic tradition, can enhance your experience and establish meaningful contacts with residents.

This chapter offers a complete guide to understanding the fundamentals of the Gaelic language, including vital phrases, language learning tools, and cultural etiquette recommendations.

Essential Gaelic Phrases

Learning a few important Gaelic phrases might help you appreciate the local culture and connect with the people of Oban. While English is commonly spoken in the area, making an effort to speak Gaelic, even if only for a few words, is highly valued by locals. Here are some key Gaelic phrases to get you started:

Madainn Mhath (MAD-In VAH): Good morning

Feasgar Math (FESH-Kur Mah): Good afternoon/evening

Oidhche Mhath (OY-khuh VAH): Good night

Tapadh Leat (TAH-Puh Let): Thank you (to one person)

Tapadh Leibh (TAH-Puh Layv): Thank you (to more than one person or in formal settings)

Slàinte Mhath (SLAN-Cha VAH): Cheers/good health

Ciamar A Tha Sibh? (KIM-Ur Uh Ha Shiv): How are you? (formal/plural)

Ciamar A Tha Thu? (KIM-Ur Uh Ha Oo): How are you? (informal/singular)

Is Mise [Your Name] (Iss MISH-Uh): I am [your name]

Fàilte (FAHL-Tuh): Welcome

Practice these phrases with locals and see how their cheeks light up with gratitude for your efforts to communicate in their language.

Language-Learning Resources

There are several resources available to help you learn Gaelic. Whether you prefer books, online classes, or language exchange programs, there is something for everyone's learning style. Here are some recommended resources to help you along the way:

Books: Boyd Robertson and Iain Taylor's "Teach Yourself Gaelic" provides a thorough approach to learning Gaelic from scratch, including grammar, vocabulary, and pronunciation. "Gaelic for Beginners" by J.D. Derrick McClure is another great resource for beginners, with clear explanations and fun exercises to help you learn.

Online Lessons: Websites such as Duolingo and Babbel provide interactive Gaelic lessons that you can complete at your own pace from the comfort of your home. These courses cover everything from fundamental phrases to advanced grammar and conversational abilities, making them suitable for both beginners and intermediate learners.

Language Exchange Programs: Participating in a language exchange program can be a fun and effective method to improve your Gaelic skills while meeting new people. Websites such as ConversationExchange.com pair language learners with native speakers for virtual language exchanges via video chat or messaging, allowing you to practice speaking Gaelic in a helpful and encouraging setting.

Local Classes And Workshops: If you're in Oban for an extended amount of time and want to immerse yourself in the local community, consider taking a Gaelic language class or workshop. Many community centers and cultural groups provide programs for beginners and intermediate learners, offering a structured learning environment as well as opportunity for hands-on experience.

Regardless of which tools you use, consistency and practice are essential for improving your Gaelic language skills. Set aside time each day to study and practice, and don't be afraid to make mistakes—every effort at speaking Gaelic moves you closer to fluency.

Cultural Etiquette Tips

As you learn about Gaelic language and culture, it's crucial to remember cultural etiquette in order to have courteous and meaningful interactions with locals.

Here are some etiquette points to bear in mind:

Respect The Language: Gaelic is an important element of Scotland's cultural history, so treat it with respect and care. Avoid making jokes or disparaging remarks about Gaelic, and express appreciation for locals who speak it.

Use Gaelic Greetings: To demonstrate respect for the language and culture, consider greeting locals with Gaelic expressions such as "madainn mhath" (good morning) or "feasgar math" (good afternoon or evening).

Be Open-Minded: Accept the contrasts between Gaelic and your own culture, and approach new experiences with an open mind and a desire to learn. Respect the local norms and traditions, even if they differ from your own.

Get Permission Before Recording Or Photographing: If you're at a Gaelic event or dealing with Gaelic speakers, always get permission before recording or photographing them. Respect their privacy and cultural sensitivity, and be aware of any limitations on photography or recording.

By following these cultural etiquette recommendations, you will demonstrate respect for the Gaelic language and culture while also fostering pleasant and lasting interactions with the Oban community.

Language Assistance Services

While English is frequently spoken in Oban, you may occasionally see Gaelic signage or hear Gaelic spoken in public places.

If you require language assistance, there are various services available to help.

Gaelic Language Applications: Install a Gaelic language application on your smartphone for quick and easy translation and pronunciation help on the move. Apps such as "Learn Gaelic" and "Gaelic Dictionary" include comprehensive dictionaries, audio pronunciations, and interactive learning aids to help you explore the language.

Language Hotlines: Some tourist information centers and cultural groups provide language hotlines or helplines, which you can contact or text for translation or interpretation services. Check with your local resources for information on available services and how to get them.

Language Schools And Tutoring Services: If you're staying in Oban for an extended amount of time or want to learn Gaelic, consider enrolling in a language school or hiring a private tutor for personalized language education. Many language schools provide flexible schedules and lesson plans to match your specific learning needs.

Local Community Centers: Oban's community centers and cultural organizations may provide Gaelic language classes, workshops, or conversation groups for students of all skill levels. These programs allow you to practice speaking Gaelic in a supportive and encouraging setting while also connecting with others who share your enthusiasm for the language.

Using these language aid programs will improve your ability to traverse Gaelic-speaking situations and interact with the Oban community.

Finally, studying basic Scottish Gaelic provides opportunities for deeper cultural awareness and genuine connections with Oban residents.

CHAPTER 14

ITINERARIES AND SAMPLE PLANS

Planning a trip to Oban can be both thrilling and daunting, especially with the abundance of things to see and do in this lovely coastal town.

Weekend Getaway

Oban's beautiful beauty and dynamic atmosphere make it ideal for a weekend getaway. With two days to explore, you may see the town's main attractions, eat wonderful food, and take in the breathtaking seaside vistas.

Here's an example agenda for a fantastic weekend away in Oban:

Day One: Arrival and Exploration

Morning: Arrive in Oban and check into your accommodations. Choose a hotel in a central location so you can easily explore the area on foot.

Begin the day with a full breakfast from a local café or bakery. To fuel your activities, eat freshly baked pastries, Scottish oatmeal, or a typical full Scottish breakfast.

Mid-Morning: Take a guided walking tour around Oban's medieval town center. Learn about the town's fascinating history, architecture, and landmarks from an expert local guide.

See McCaig's Tower, a stunning structure standing atop Battery Hill. Climb the steps to the top for a panoramic view of Oban Bay and its neighboring islands.

Lunch-Time: Spend a relaxing lunch at one of Oban's seafood eateries or traditional pubs. Try local favorites like freshly caught seafood, haggis, or substantial stews with a pint of Scottish ale.

Afternoon: Take a guided tour of the Oban Distillery and learn about the whisky-making process. Learn about the distillery's history and manufacturing process, and try a variety of superb single malts.

Take a stroll down the scenic esplanade and enjoy views of Oban Bay, which is studded with fishing boats and yachts. Take photographs of the landmark McCaig's Tower standing over the town.

Evening: Enjoy a wonderful evening at a beachfront restaurant that overlooks Oban Bay. Enjoy a delicious seafood feast with locally sourced ingredients and freshly cooked dishes.

Wrap off the day with a leisurely stroll down the harborfront promenade, taking in the dazzling lights of the town and the serene serenity of the sea at sunset.

Day Two: Outdoor Adventures and Culinary Delights

Morning: Begin the day with a brisk hike or seaside walk along one of Oban's picturesque pathways. For breathtaking scenery and pure sea air, take the Oban to Dunollie Castle hike or the Ganavan Sands circle.

Alternatively, take a guided sea kayaking adventure to discover Oban's craggy coastline and hidden bays. Paddle past steep cliffs, sea caves, and marine creatures while taking in the natural splendor of the area.

Lunch-Time: Have a picnic in nature or a light lunch at a coastal café or deli. Sample exquisite sandwiches, locally sourced salads, and handmade desserts to fuel your afternoon travels.

Afternoon: Visit the Scottish SEA creatures Sanctuary to learn about and interact with marine creatures. Explore exhibits featuring seals, otters, sharks, and seahorses, as well as information on regional conservation activities.

Take a picturesque drive or ferry journey to the adjacent Isle of Kerrera to see island life. Explore historic places such as Gylen Castle, meander along isolated beaches, and take in the stunning vistas of Oban and its neighboring islands.

Evening: Return to Oban and have a fantastic meal in a fine-dining restaurant or comfortable cafe. Enjoy gourmet meals made with locally produced ingredients and combined with good wines or craft beers.

Wrap up your weekend getaway with a sunset boat around Oban Bay. Relax on deck as you sail past stunning islands, lighthouses, and coastal cliffs, taking in the peace and beauty of the Scottish coast.

Cultural Immersion

A cultural immersion schedule provides guests with a unique opportunity to discover Oban's historical landmarks, museums, and cultural attractions, allowing them to have a better grasp of the town's rich culture and tradition. Discover Oban's dynamic cultural scene by immersing yourself in its unique arts, traditions, and cuisine.

Here's an example itinerary for a cultural immersion trip in Oban.

Day One: Heritage And History.

Morning: Begin your cultural immersion by visiting the Dunollie Museum, Castle, and Grounds. Explore the medieval castle ruins, stroll through the picturesque gardens, and visit the museum's displays on Oban's Gaelic roots and maritime history.

Mid-Morning: Participate in a traditional Gaelic language and music workshop at the Dunollie Learning Center. Learn simple Gaelic phrases, practice playing traditional Scottish instruments such as the bagpipes or fiddle, and immerse yourself in Gaelic culture's rich traditions.

Lunch-Time: Have a traditional Scottish meal in a local restaurant or pub. Try regional favorites such as cullen skink (smoked haddock chowder), haggis neeps and tatties, or Scotch broth, along with freshly baked bread and a drink of whisky.

Afternoon: Visit the Oban War and Peace Museum to learn about the town's involvement in World War II and contributions to the war effort. Explore exhibits illustrating Oban's maritime heritage, wartime artifacts, and personal stories from local inhabitants.

Evening: Attend a traditional Scottish ceilidh (pronounced "kay-lee") at a nearby venue or community center. Participate in the exciting music and dance as you learn traditional Scottish ceilidh dances such as the Gay Gordons, Strip the Willow, and Dashing White Sergeant.

Day Two: Arts and culture

Morning: Visit the Rockfield Centre, a lively community arts complex set in a historic old school building. Browse art galleries, participate in workshops and performances, and interact with local artists and craftspeople.

Mid-Morning: Enroll in a traditional Scottish cooking class at a nearby culinary school or community center. Expert chefs will teach you how to make iconic Scottish meals such as haggis, stovies, cranachan, and shortbread.

Lunch-Time: Have a leisurely lunch at a classic tearoom or café, sampling homemade soups, sandwiches, and pastries. Enjoy sweet delights such as scones with clotted cream and jam, Victoria sponge cake, and traditional Scottish tablet.

Afternoon: Take a guided tour of the Oban Distillery and sample its products. Learn about the whisky-making process, from malted barley to cask aging, and drink a variety of premium single malts, blends, and limited editions.

Visit the Oban Phoenix Cinema, a magnificent art deco movie theater that dates back to 1935. Watch a classic film or an independent film while taking in the nostalgic atmosphere of this cherished local icon.

Evening: Go to a traditional Scottish music concert or a folk music session at a nearby pub or music venue. Listen to live performances of classic Scottish songs, fiddle tunes, and ballads, and join in the fun as musicians and residents band together to celebrate Scotland's musical history.

Conclusion: Oban has something for everyone, whether you want a weekend escape full of outdoor adventures and scenic beauty or a cultural immersion experience rich in history, art, and culture. By following these sample itineraries and plans, you'll be able to visit Oban's major sights, experience its culinary pleasures, and immerse yourself in the lively culture and tradition.

When planning your vacation, keep an eye out for any seasonal events, festivals, or special exhibitions that will be taking place during your stay, as they can offer an added layer of excitement and enrichment to your experience. Whether you choose to go on a weekend excursion or immerse yourself in local culture, Oban's charm and beauty will leave an indelible effect on you.

By utilizing these tools and implementing them into your travel plans, you'll be well-prepared for an outstanding trip to Oban, where adventure, culture, and beauty await at every step.

Outdoor Adventure

Oban, hidden amongst breathtaking natural landscapes and coastline vistas, is an outdoor enthusiast's dream. There are plenty of outdoor adventures to be had in and around Oban, ranging from rough hiking paths to thrilling aquatic activities.

Here's an example itinerary for an exciting outdoor excursion in Oban.

Day One: Exploring the Great Outdoors

Morning: Begin your day with a substantial breakfast at your hotel or one of Oban's quaint cafes. Prepare for a day of outdoor exploring ahead.

Take a morning trek through the nearby Glencruitten Forest, which features old woodlands and lovely pathways. Choose from a variety of difficulty levels, including the Glencruitten Loop and the summit trail to Dunstaffnage Castle for panoramic views of Oban Bay.

Mid-Morning: For thrill seekers, engage on a sea kayaking excursion around Oban's rough shoreline. Join a guided trip or hire kayaks independently to explore sea caves, secluded coves, and coastal cliffs while admiring the breathtaking scenery and marine fauna.

Lunch-Time: Have a picnic lunch in nature, or stop at a lovely site overlooking the sea to eat sandwiches, snacks, and local specialties. Take in the fresh air and peacefulness of your surroundings as you prepare for your afternoon adventures.

Afternoon: Head to adjacent Kerrera Island for an afternoon of exploration and outdoor activities. Hike or cycle over the island's picturesque pathways, stopping to admire historic sites such as Gylen Castle and take in panoramic views of Oban and the neighboring islands.

Alternatively, take a guided wildlife-watching cruise to see seals, dolphins, seabirds, and other marine species in their natural environment. Learn about local conservation efforts and marine habitats from qualified guides while experiencing the excitement of wildlife encounters.

Evening: Return to Oban and have a relaxing stroll along the town's gorgeous waterfront promenade. Take in the sunset over Oban Bay and photograph the gorgeous skies reflected in the tranquil waters.

Treat yourself to a great evening at a seafood restaurant or traditional pub, where you can appreciate freshly caught fish and locally produced delicacies coupled with fine wines or craft beer. Reflect on the day's adventures and make plans for further outdoor activities tomorrow.

Day Two: Coastal Excursions and Water-related Thrills

Morning: Get up early and take a wildlife-watching boat cruise to the adjacent islands of Mull, Staffa, or Iona. Keep a watch out for whales, dolphins, puffins, and other marine species as you sail through pristine waterways and visit secluded islands and sea caves.

Mid-Morning: For those who prefer a slower pace, take a beautiful drive along the Argyll Coastal Route to discover hidden beaches, lovely villages, and ancient sites. Stop at viewpoints and photo locations along the trip to capture spectacular coastline views and scenic landscapes.

Lunch-Time: Have a seafood lunch in a beachfront restaurant or beachside cafe, sampling freshly caught fish and shellfish cooked in traditional Scottish and foreign methods. For the ideal beach dining experience, pair your meal with a cold white wine or a local craft ale.

Afternoon: Round out your outdoor experiences with an afternoon spent snorkeling or diving in Oban's crystal-clear seas. Diving or snorkeling with expert guides allows you to explore underwater rock formations, kelp forests, and marine animal habitats.

Alternatively, take a sailing tour or boat charter to see Oban's coastal waters from a new angle. Sail by rocky cliffs, secluded islands, and hidden bays while enjoying the excitement of sailing and the peace of the sea.

Evening: Wrap up your outdoor excursion with a sunset boat around Oban Bay, taking in the golden hues of the setting sun and the tranquil serenity of the coastal scenery. Relax on deck with a glass of champagne or whisky, toasting to a day of unforgettable experiences.

Have a goodbye meal at a seaside restaurant, eating your favorite seafood dishes and local specialties while reflecting on your outdoor excursions in Oban.

Before leaving this coastal jewel, raise a drink to nature's beauty and the delight of exploring.

Family-Friendly Trip

Oban has a variety of family-friendly attractions and activities to keep people of all ages entertained. Everyone can enjoy activities ranging from wildlife encounters to interactive museums.

Here's an example agenda for a fun family trip to Oban:

Day One: Family Fun and Exploration.

Morning: Begin your day with a visit to the Scottish SEA LIFE Sanctuary, where families can see beautiful aquatic species and learn about conservation initiatives. Explore interactive exhibits, see feeding demonstrations, and get up close and personal with seals, otters, sharks, and other wildlife.

Afterward, take a leisurely stroll around Oban's esplanade, stopping to enjoy the playgrounds and picnic spaces that overlook the bay. Allow the youngsters to burn off some energy while the parents rest and take in the breathtaking scenery.

Mid-Morning: Visit Oban Chocolate Company for a delicious treat and a hands-on chocolate-making workshop. Allow the kids to express their creativity while decorating their own chocolates and indulging in delectable artisanal delicacies.

Lunch-Time: Have a family lunch at a local cafe or restaurant, trying kid-friendly options like fish & chips, burgers, or pizza. Choose a location with outside seats to soak up the sun and enjoy al fresco dining.

Afternoon: Spend the afternoon at Oban Bay Play, a wonderful indoor play facility with soft play sections, slides, climbing frames, and interactive activities. Allow the kids to run, jump, and play to their hearts' content while the parents unwind with a cup of coffee at the cafe.

Evening: Take the family out to dinner at a family-friendly restaurant or pub, where you can relax together and sample a range of foods to suit everyone's taste. Finish your day with a leisurely stroll along the harborfront promenade, soaking in the sights and sounds of Oban at night.

Day Two: Nature and Adventure

Morning: Begin your day with Sealife Adventures, where families may go on an exciting wildlife-watching boat excursion in search of seals, dolphins, whales, and seabirds. Learn about the local marine ecosystem and conservation activities from trained guides while having intimate experiences with marine animals.

After the boat excursion, visit Ganavan Sands for a morning of beachcombing, sandcastle building, and seaside activities. Allow the youngsters to play in the surf, discover rock pools, and enjoy the fresh sea air and beautiful coastal landscape.

Mid-Morning: For families with older children, take a guided sea kayaking tour around Oban's rough shoreline. Paddle past sea cliffs, caves, and hidden coves while learning about marine life and coastal ecosystems from expert guides.

Lunch-Time: Have a picnic lunch on the beach or at a lovely viewpoint that overlooks the water. Pack a picnic basket with sandwiches, snacks, and cold beverages, and take a break to refuel and rejuvenate before your afternoon adventures.

Afternoon: Spend the afternoon exploring Dunollie Castle and Grounds, a magnificent castle set on a rock above Oban Bay. Take a guided tour of the castle remains, walk around the picturesque grounds, and admire the panoramic views of the surrounding coastline and islands. Discover the castle's interesting history and the strong Clan MacDougall, who once governed this land.

Evening: Wrap up your family excursion with a guided tour and whisky tasting at Oban Distillery. While adults experience Oban's well-known single malt whisky, children may enjoy non-alcoholic beverages and learn about the whisky-making process from knowledgeable guides.

After the tour, visit a nearby restaurant for a goodbye dinner featuring substantial Scottish cooking and locally produced ingredients. Toast to a memorable family vacation in Oban and share your finest memories and experiences.

By following these sample itineraries and plans, you can make amazing moments with your loved ones while discovering the beauty and charm of Oban. Oban has something for everyone, whether you want to go on an adventure, have fun with your family, or learn about culture.

Using these resources and adapting your itinerary to your family's interests and preferences will prepare you for a great family-friendly adventure in Oban, where fun, laughter, and exploration await at every step.

Budget Travel

Oban, with its breathtaking natural beauty and rich cultural legacy, provides several options for budget tourists to discover and enjoy without breaking the bank.

Here's a sample plan for exploring Oban on a budget, including reasonable lodging alternatives and free or low-cost activities.

Day One: Exploring Oban on a Budget

Morning: Begin your day with a low-cost breakfast at a local bakery or cafe, where you may eat freshly baked pastries, oatmeal, or a substantial Scottish breakfast without going overboard.

After breakfast, take a self-guided walking tour of Oban's historic town center. Explore the picturesque streets lined with colorful houses, visit the local stores and boutiques, and see sights like as McCaig's Tower and Oban Distillery.

Mid-Morning: Discover the town's maritime heritage and military history at the Oban War and Peace Museum, which is free to explore. Explore exhibits displaying antiques, photographs, and memorabilia from Oban's history, including its participation in World War II and its link to the sea.

Lunch-Time: Have a low-cost lunch at a local deli, sandwich shop, or takeaway restaurant, where you may try economical and excellent Scottish staples such as fish and chips, haggis, or a nourishing soup and sandwich combo.

Alternatively, pack a picnic lunch and head to one of Oban's scenic vistas or parks to eat outside while admiring panoramic views of the town and coastline.

Afternoon: Spend the afternoon touring Oban's free or low-cost attractions, including the Oban Distillery Visitor Centre. While the distillery tour has a minor entrance price, it provides an interesting insight into the whisky-making process and concludes with a complimentary sampling of Oban whisky.

Evening: For dinner, choose a neighborhood bar or restaurant that offers low-cost menu alternatives, daily specials, or early bird discounts. While mixing with locals and fellow travelers, indulge in classic pub grub or traditional Scottish cuisine.

After supper, take a leisurely stroll down Oban's waterfront promenade to enjoy the spectacular sunset views over the bay and watch the fishing boats return to the harbor.

Day Two: Outdoor Adventures on a Budget

Morning: Begin your day with a low-cost breakfast at your hotel or a nearby cafe, preparing for a day of outdoor adventures.

Pack a picnic lunch and visit one of Oban's gorgeous outdoor attractions, such as Ganavan Sands or Pulpit Hill. Spend the morning hiking, picnicking, or simply resting in the stunning Scottish countryside.

Mid-Morning: Take a guided wildlife-watching boat cruise to see seals, seagulls, and other marine animals in their natural environment. While there is a cost for boat cruises, they are good value for money and deliver spectacular wildlife encounters and scenery.

Lunch-Time: Enjoy your picnic lunch at a lovely location overlooking the sea or countryside, soaking up the quiet and beauty of your surroundings. Alternatively, return to Oban and lunch at a low-cost cafe or restaurant serving hearty and reasonable meals.

Afternoon: Spend the day seeing some of Oban's outdoor attractions, including Dunollie Castle and Grounds. While there is a little admission price to visit the castle remains and grounds, it is well worth it for the breathtaking vistas and medieval atmosphere.

Evening: Finish your budget-friendly journey with a casual dinner at a nearby pub or takeaway restaurant, where you can eat good food without breaking the bank. Reflect on your outdoor adventures and memorable experiences in Oban as you choose your next low-cost vacation destination.

Solo Traveler's Guide

Oban is a welcome place for lone travelers, with several options for exploration, leisure, and mingling.

Day One: Solo Exploration and Discovery.

Morning: Begin your day with a solo breakfast at a local cafe or bakery, where you can eat leisurely while organizing your day's activities. Take advantage of the opportunity to people-watch and enjoy the atmosphere of Oban's lively streets.

Mid-Morning: Take a self-guided walking tour of Oban's historic town center, taking in the sights and sounds of this quaint seaside town at your leisure. Visit landmarks such as McCaig's Tower, Oban Distillery, and the Oban War and Peace Museum.

Lunch-Time: Have a solo lunch at a quaint cafe or restaurant, enjoying in delectable Scottish food and local delicacies. Choose a window seat or an outdoor table to enjoy views of the busy streets and harbor while dining.

Afternoon: Spend the afternoon seeing Oban's outdoor attractions, including Dunollie Castle and Grounds and the picturesque vistas along the Argyll Coastal Route. Take your time wandering through the gardens, hiking along seaside trails, and photographing the stunning surroundings.

Evening: For dinner, go to a nearby restaurant or pub and enjoy a lone meal while taking in the vibrant ambiance and possibly starting up a conversation with other diners or pleasant locals. Take advantage of the opportunity to meet new people and share your trip experiences.

Day Two: Outdoor Adventure and Relaxation

Morning: Begin the day with an early morning trek or nature walk along one of Oban's picturesque trails or seaside walks. Immerse yourself in the grandeur of Scotland's countryside while enjoying the isolation and tranquility of the natural surroundings.

Mid-Morning: Take a guided wildlife-watching boat excursion around Oban's coastal waterways to see seals, dolphins, seabirds, and other marine life. Accept the opportunity to connect with nature and learn about the local environment from experienced guides.

Lunch-Time: Have a solo picnic lunch at a lovely location overlooking the sea or countryside, savoring the solitude and quiet of your surroundings. Before continuing your expedition, take some time to relax, recover, and reflect on your previous outdoor activities.

Afternoon: Spend the day exploring more of Oban's outdoor attractions or practicing solo relaxation and self-care. Enjoy a spa treatment, a yoga class, or a leisurely stroll along the waterfront promenade while admiring the tranquility of the coastal surroundings.

Evening: End your solo excursion with a peaceful meal at a local restaurant or takeaway bistro, relishing the flavors of Scottish cuisine and reflecting on your time in Oban. Raise a glass to your solo travels and the connections you created as you plan your next solo excursion.

Following these sample itineraries and plans allows solitary visitors to appreciate the beauty, charm, and hospitality of Oban while having the freedom and flexibility to explore at their own speed. Oban offers plenty to offer lone visitors seeking adventure, relaxation, or connection.

Romantic Getaways

Oban, with its stunning surroundings, charming seaside ambiance, and romantic allure, is ideal for couples looking for a romantic escape. From gorgeous walks along the waterfront to intimate dinners overlooking the sea, here's an example itinerary for a romantic getaway to Oban:

Day One: Romantic exploration and discovery.

Morning: Begin your romantic holiday with a leisurely breakfast for two at a cozy cafe or bakery, complete with freshly made pastries, gourmet coffee, and other delectable delicacies. Take your time with each bite and enjoy the lovely aura of the morning.

Mid-Morning: Take a romantic stroll along Oban's waterfront promenade with your spouse. Enjoy the breathtaking views of the bay, breathe in the fresh sea air, and take a moment to enjoy the colorful fishing boats and yachts that line the harbor.

Lunch-Time: Have a romantic lunch at a waterfront restaurant or cafe, where you can eat outside on a terrace or balcony overlooking the sea. Enjoy fresh seafood, locally sourced delicacies, and a glass of wine as you celebrate your love and experiences in Oban.

Afternoon: Spend the afternoon discovering Oban's romantic attractions and hidden jewels, such as the peaceful gardens of Dunollie Castle and Grounds and the isolated beaches of Ganavan Sands. Take your time walking hand in hand, pausing to appreciate the natural beauty and historic landmarks along the way.

Evening: For a romantic supper, reserve a seat at a fine dining restaurant or upmarket café renowned for its great cuisine and cozy atmosphere. Enjoy a romantic supper for two, savoring each meal and engaging in meaningful conversation as you celebrate your love and time together in Oban.

Day Two: Romantic Adventures and Relaxation

Morning: Begin your second day by having a romantic breakfast in bed, ordering room service, or making a homemade breakfast for your companion. Enjoy a leisurely meal together, nestled up in the luxury of your accommodations, before embarking on your day's adventures.

Mid-Morning: Take a romantic boat tour of Oban's coastal waterways, where you may discover hidden coves, sea caves, and remote islands with your spouse. A private charter or small group tour will provide a more intimate and personalized experience.

Lunch-Time: Have a picnic lunch for two on a private beach or clifftop viewpoint, where you can relish a gourmet buffet of local cheeses, charcuterie, and fresh fruits while taking in the spectacular views of the sea and surroundings.

Afternoon: In the afternoon, indulge in a couples' spa treatment or relaxation session at a local wellness center or luxury resort. Relax together with massages, facials, or aromatherapy treatments to soothe and recharge your bodies and minds.

Evening: Round out your romantic holiday with a private sunset cruise or coastal walk, where you can watch the sun sink below the horizon in a blaze of hues, throwing a beautiful glow over the water and sky. Reflect on your time together in Oban and treasure the memories you've made as you prepare to return home feeling refreshed and renewed.

Couples can enjoy a romantic escape to Oban with this sample itinerary, which includes amazing experiences, cherished moments, and unlimited opportunities for romance and connection.

Oban is the ideal setting for a memorable romantic trip, whether you're celebrating a special occasion or simply looking for quality time together.

CHAPTER 15

SAFETY TIPS FOR VISITORS

Safety is essential when visiting any destination, and Oban is no different. While this picturesque coastal town has a welcoming and friendly environment, tourists must exercise caution to protect their safety and well-being during their stay.

In this chapter, we'll go over general safety considerations, emergency contacts, health and medical facilities, and the value of travel insurance and documentation.

General Safety Precautions

Stay Informed: Before embarking on your trip to Oban, extensively investigate the area to become acquainted with local customs, laws, and any hazards. Keep up with any travel alerts or updates from authoritative sources.

Stay Vigilant: While Oban is typically a safe place, it is critical to exercise caution, particularly in popular tourist areas and during peak tourist seasons. Always keep a watch on your stuff and be alert of your surroundings.

Watch The Weather: Weather in Scotland can be variable, with rain, wind, and fog occurring throughout the year. Check the weather forecast on a frequent basis and prepare for changing conditions by wearing in layers and carrying appropriate gear.

Respect Nature: Oban's natural landscapes are its most appealing feature, yet they can also offer risks if not explored with prudence. When exploring outdoor regions, stick to defined pathways, obey warning signs, and avoid wandering too close to cliff edges or hazardous ground.

Be Hydrated And Nourished: Whether you're hiking, touring, or doing other outdoor activities, it's critical to be hydrated and nourished all day. Bring water and food with you, especially if you plan to spend long periods of time outside.

Use Caution Near Water: Oban's coastline is breathtaking, but it can also be dangerous, with powerful currents and unexpected tides. When swimming, kayaking, or participating in water-based activities, use caution and always obey lifeguard directions and safety rules.

Travel With A Companion: Whenever possible, travel with a companion or in a group, particularly while visiting rural or unknown locations. Having someone with you might add an extra degree of security and support in the event of an emergency.

Follow Local Laws And Customs: Respect the local laws, customs, and cultural sensitivity during your stay to Oban. Familiarize oneself with any applicable rules or restrictions, such as alcohol consumption legislation and designated smoking places.

Emergency Contacts

In the event of an emergency during your stay in Oban, you must have access to necessary contact information for local authorities and emergency agencies.

Here are some crucial figures to keep handy:

Emergency Services (Police, Fire, Ambulance): Call 999

Oban Police Station: +44 (0) 1631 510500.

Oban Hospital: +44 (0) 1631 563491.

Also, if you're staying at a hotel or lodging in Oban, ask about their emergency procedures and contact information for onsite staff or management.

Health Care Facilities

Oban has various medical facilities and pharmacies where visitors can obtain medical care if necessary. These facilities offer a wide range of services, including general healthcare, emergency treatment, and prescription drugs. Some important health and medical facilities in Oban are:

Lorn And Islands Hospital: Situated on the outskirts of Oban, Lorn and Islands Hospital offers a wide range of healthcare services, including accident and emergency treatment, outpatient clinics, and diagnostic services.

Pharmacies: There are several pharmacies in central Oban where visitors can buy over-the-counter medications, prescription drugs, and medical supplies. Pharmacists can also offer advise and guidance on minor medical conditions.

General Practitioners (GPs): Visitors who require non-emergency medical treatment can contact their local GP or healthcare provider. Many GP practices in Oban accept both appointments and walk-ins.

Dentists: If you have a dental emergency, you can go to one of Oban's local dental practices. Dental examinations, emergency dental treatment, and routine operations are all possible services.

Before traveling to Oban, make sure you have comprehensive travel insurance that covers medical emergencies and repatriation. Make sure you understand your insurance policy's coverage limits, exclusions, and emergency contact information.

Travel Insurance And Documents

Travel insurance is a vital part of trip planning since it provides financial security and peace of mind in the event of unforeseen events or emergencies.

When visiting Oban, it is critical to have full travel insurance coverage, which includes:

Medical Coverage: If you become ill or injured while traveling, travel insurance can pay for medical expenditures, hospitalization, and emergency medical evacuation or repatriation.

Travel Cancellation Or Interruption: Travel insurance can compensate you for non-refundable travel expenses in the event of trip cancellation, interruption, or delays caused by insured events such as illness, injury, or natural disasters.

Lost Or Stolen possessions: Travel insurance can protect you against lost, stolen, or damaged luggage, personal possessions, and travel papers like passports and visas.

Emergency Support Services: Many travel insurance policies provide 24-hour emergency support, which includes access to medical professionals, travel aid, and coordination of emergency medical evacuations.

Before getting travel insurance, carefully read the policy coverage, terms, and conditions to ensure that it suits your unique requirements and provides appropriate protection for your trip to Oban. Keep a copy of your travel insurance policy and emergency contact information on hand at all times during your visit.

Finally, prioritizing safety and preparedness is critical for a pleasurable and worry-free trip to Oban. You may enjoy everything Oban has to offer with confidence and peace of mind if you take general safety precautions, are familiar with emergency contacts and medical services, and have proper travel insurance coverage.

CHAPTER 16

SUSTAINABLE TRAVEL IN OBAN

Sustainable travel is becoming more essential as we work to reduce our environmental effect while preserving the natural beauty and cultural legacy of places like Oban.

In this chapter, we'll look at eco-friendly lodging options, responsible tourist practices, conservation activities, and community projects that encourage sustainability in Oban.

Environmentally Friendly Accommodation Options

Travelers to Oban can choose eco-friendly accommodations that stress sustainability and environmental responsibility.

These lodgings are dedicated to lowering their carbon footprint, saving resources, and helping local communities.

Here are some environmentally friendly hotel choices to consider:

Green Hotels And Lodges: Many Oban hotels and lodges have adopted environmentally friendly practices such as energy-efficient lighting, water conservation measures, and waste reduction programs. Look for lodging that has been accredited by sustainable tourism programs or has acquired eco-friendly certifications.

Eco-Lodges And Eco-Retreats: For travelers looking for a more immersive eco-friendly experience, eco-lodges and eco-retreats provide sustainable lodging in natural locations. These sites frequently use renewable energy sources, encourage biodiversity protection, and provide environmental education programs.

Farm Stays And Rural Retreats: Staying in a farm stay or rural retreat on the outskirts of Oban allows you to gain firsthand experience with sustainable living. These lodgings offer opportunity to practice organic farming, learn about local food production, and support rural communities.

Hostels And Guesthouses: Budget-conscious tourists can find eco-friendly lodging options in Oban. Look for hotels that value sustainability by offering recycling programs, energy-efficient appliances, and locally produced amenities.

Travelers can reduce their environmental effect by staying in Oban's eco-friendly accommodations while also supporting businesses dedicated to sustainability and responsible tourism.

Responsible Tourist Practices

Responsible tourism refers to traveling in a way that supports local people, honors cultural heritage, and reduces negative environmental impacts. Visitors to Oban can engage in a variety of responsible tourism behaviors that benefit both the place and its inhabitants. Here are some recommendations for responsible travel to Oban:

Support Local Businesses: When dining out, shopping, or scheduling tours and activities, choose local businesses that benefit the local economy and employ locals. Choose eateries that use locally sourced ingredients, and buy mementos at artisanal shops and craft markets.

Respect Cultural Legacy: Oban has a rich cultural legacy that includes Gaelic traditions, historical sites, and indigenous communities. Respect local customs, traditions, and sacred locations, and look for opportunities to learn about and interact with the local culture through cultural events, festivals, and guided tours.

Minimize Environmental Impact: Practice sustainable behaviors including conserving water and electricity, reducing trash, and adopting eco-friendly transportation. When possible, use walking, cycling, or public transportation, and look for eco-friendly tours and activities that promote conservation and environmental care.

Leave No Trace: When exploring Oban's natural environments, adhere to the Leave No Trace principles by removing any waste, staying on designated pathways, and avoiding damage to vegetation and wildlife habitats. Maintain a safe distance while viewing and photographing wildlife. Avoid disruptive activity.

By adopting responsible tourism habits, visitors may positively contribute to the well-being of Oban's communities and environment while also having meaningful and authentic travel experiences.

Conservation Efforts

Oban is home to a variety of ecosystems, including coastal habitats, marine environments, and protected natural areas, which are the focus of conservation efforts to preserve biodiversity and ecological balance. Several organizations and activities in Oban are committed to conservation and environmental stewardship:

Marine Conservation: Oban's coastal waters are rich with marine life, including seals, dolphins, and sea birds. Marine conservation organizations safeguard these delicate habitats by doing research, monitoring, and advocating for marine conservation regulations.

Nature Reserves And Protected Areas: Oban is surrounded by breathtaking natural landscapes including as woods, ponds, and mountains that are recognized as nature reserves or conservation areas. These protected areas serve as critical habitat for species while also providing opportunities for outdoor leisure and nature-based tourism.

Wildlife Rehabilitation Centers: In Oban, injured or orphaned wildlife are cared for and rehabilitated at wildlife rehabilitation centers before being released back into the wild.

These facilities also serve an important role in teaching the public about wildlife protection and environmental concerns.

Community Conservation Projects: Oban's local communities actively participate in conservation efforts through activities such as beach cleanups, tree planting events, and habitat restoration. These programs engage both residents and visitors in hands-on conservation activities, instilling a sense of environmental care.

Travelers can help to safeguard Oban's natural resources and biodiversity for future generations by volunteering, making donations, or participating in eco-friendly tours and activities.

Community Initiatives

In Oban, community initiatives play an important role in improving sustainability, encouraging community engagement, and empowering residents. These efforts emphasize diverse aspects of community development, environmental protection, and cultural preservation:

Community Gardens And Allotments: Community gardens and allotments allow locals to cultivate their own fruits, vegetables, and flowers, increasing local food production, lowering food miles, and cultivating a sense of community connectedness.

Cultural Festivals And Events: Oban offers a number of cultural festivals and events throughout the year, which celebrate local customs, music, art, and cuisine. These events not only highlight the region's distinct cultural legacy, but also benefit local artists, entertainers, and businesses.

Community-Owned Enterprises: Some Oban businesses and services are locally owned and operated, with earnings reinvested in community projects and initiatives. Supporting community-owned firms positively benefits the community's economic well-being and helps to sustain local livelihoods.

Environmental Education Programs: Oban's environmental education programs and projects seek to create knowledge about environmental issues, encourage sustainable living practices, and empower people to take action to protect the environment. These activities frequently cater to schools, community organizations, and the general public, offering opportunity for hands-on learning and interaction.

Participating in community activities allows visitors to engage with locals, learn about the destination's culture and way of life, and contribute to positive social and environmental change in Oban.

To summarize, sustainable travel in Oban includes a variety of behaviors and projects aiming at reducing environmental effect, helping local communities, and maintaining the destination's natural and cultural legacy. Travelers may make a difference in Oban by staying in eco-friendly accommodations, practicing responsible tourism, supporting conservation efforts, and participating in community initiatives.

CHAPTER 17

PHOTOGRAPHY GUIDE

Photography is an excellent method to capture memories and highlight the beauty of Oban's scenery, sites, and culture. In this chapter, we'll look at photography ideas and techniques to help you take beautiful photographs of Oban.

This chapter will provide you with the knowledge and skills you need to capture fascinating photographs of Oban, from discovering the ideal photo places to mastering lighting and composition, selecting the correct equipment, and enhancing your photos through editing and post-processing.

Best Photospots

McCraig's Tower: Perched on a hill overlooking Oban, the tower provides panoramic views of the town, harbor, and neighboring islands. Capture amazing sunrise and sunset photos from this vantage point, with the sun's warm glow illuminating the area.

Oban Bay: The scenic bay of Oban is a popular destination for photographers, with opportunities to capture reflections of boats, colorful buildings along the waterfront, and distant hills beyond. Experiment with different angles and compositions to get unique views of the bay.

Dunollie Castle: Dunollie Castle, which dates back to the 12th century, provides a striking backdrop for photography, especially during golden hour, when the soft light bathes the ruins in a warm glow. Explore the castle grounds to discover unique compositions and perspectives.

Ganavan Sands: This gorgeous beach just outside Oban provides limitless options for beachscape photography, with its golden sands, rocky outcrops, and vistas of the surrounding coastline. To produce dreamy seascapes, photograph reflections in damp sand or use long exposure techniques.

Island Hopping: Take a ferry or boat cruise to the surrounding islands of Mull, Iona, and Staffa, where you'll find rough coasts, historic ruins, and plenty of wildlife. These islands provide several photo options, ranging from stunning sea cliffs to calm beaches and historical landmarks.

Lighting And Composition Tips

Golden Hour: The hours immediately following sunrise and before sunset, known as the golden hour, provide soft, warm light great for photography. Take advantage of this lovely time of day to photograph landscapes in golden hues with lengthy, dramatic shadows.

Rule Of Thirds: The rule of thirds might help you compose visually appealing photos. Divide your frame into thirds, both horizontally and vertically, and place your main subject or focal point at the junction of these lines to create a balanced composition.

Leading Lines: Look for natural or man-made components that can draw the viewer's attention to the landscape, such as highways, paths, or shorelines. These leading lines give depth and texture to your images while also conveying a sense of movement or direction.

Foreground Interest: Use items in the foreground of your photographs to offer depth and context to the scene. This could range from rocks or flowers in a landscape photo to people or objects in a street setting. Experiment with various foreground elements to make visually appealing compositions.

Experiment With Viewpoints: Don't be scared to try out multiple viewpoints and angles to find the most appealing composition. Get low to the ground for a unique perspective, or climb to a higher vantage point for a more elevated vision. Changing your perspective can radically alter the appearance and feel of your photographs.

Equipment Recommendations

Camera: Whether you use a DSLR, mirrorless camera, or smartphone, select a camera that is appropriate for your skill level and photography goals. While professional-grade cameras provide greater control and image quality, many smartphones now include superior camera technology capable of producing amazing images.

Lenses: Choose lenses that match your photographic style and themes of interest. A versatile zoom lens is perfect for capturing a wide range of scenes, whilst prime lenses provide higher image quality and low-light capabilities. Consider purchasing a wide-angle lens for landscapes and a telephoto lens for animals and close-up photography.

Tripod: A robust tripod is crucial for capturing clear, blur-free photographs, especially in low-light circumstances or with slow shutter speeds. Look for a tripod that is lightweight, compact, and simple to assemble, with adjustable legs and a sturdy mounting plate for your camera.

Filters: Consider purchasing a collection of filters to improve your photographs and generate creative effects in camera. Polarizing filters decrease glare and reflections; neutral density filters enable long exposure photography; and graduated neutral density filters balance exposure in high-contrast subjects.

Accessories: Don't forget to bring additional batteries, memory cards, lens cleaning materials, and a camera bag or backpack to safeguard your equipment while touring Oban.

Editing And Post-Processing Techniques

Adjust Exposure And Contrast: Use editing tools to change the exposure, contrast, and brightness settings in your photographs to improve the overall tonal range and contrast. Adjust the highlights, shadows, and midtones in your photos to bring out details and add depth.

Crop And Straighten: Crop your photographs to improve composition and eliminate distracting things from the frame. Straighten horizons and lines to make your photographs more visually attractive.

Color Enhancement: Adjust the saturation, vibrance, and hue levels in your images to improve their color. Make selective color tweaks to highlight specific colors or create a consistent color palette throughout your photographs.

Sharpen And Reduce Noise: Use sharpening and noise reduction techniques to enhance the clarity and sharpness of your photographs. Masking allows you to selectively sharpen regions of detail while leaving smoother sections of the image alone.

Experiment With Filters And Presets: Use creative filters and presets to give your images artistic effects and stylish styles. To add a distinct aesthetic to your photographs, experiment with black and white conversions, antique film effects, or creative color grading.

By following these photography ideas and techniques, you will be able to create breathtaking photographs of Oban's landscapes, sites, and culture, capturing memories for years to come. To realize your maximum photographic potential, experiment with varied locations, lighting, and composition, and enjoy the creative process.

Oban provides an abundance of opportunity for photography enthusiasts to perfect their abilities and capture the beauty of this quaint seaside town, whether they are seasoned professionals or novices.

CHAPTER 18

INSIDER TIPS FROM LOCALS

Exploring a place like Oban entails more than just visiting well-known attractions; it's also about discovering hidden jewels, off-the-beaten-path attractions, and local secrets that only insiders are aware of.

In this chapter, we'll give exclusive advice from locals to help you find the true essence of Oban and enjoy it like a local. From hidden jewels and lesser-known sights to insider eating recommendations and local secrets, these suggestions will enrich your Oban experience and allow you to dive deeper into the heart of this picturesque seaside town.

Hidden Gems

Pulpit Hill: Nestled on the outskirts of Oban, Pulpit Hill provides breathtaking panoramic views of the town, harbor, and surrounding landscape. Take a leisurely trek to the summit and enjoy a picnic while admiring the spectacular views.

Gallanach Beach: Escape the throng and explore the tranquil beauty of Gallanach Beach, which is just a short drive from the town center. This hidden gem has immaculate sands, brilliant blue waters, and unobstructed views of the surrounding islands.

Dunstaffnage Castle: Go beyond the well-trodden tourist path to see Dunstaffnage Castle, a medieval fortification steeped in history. Wander around the old ruins, ascend the spiral staircase to the battlements, and experience life centuries ago.

Ganavan Sands Nature Reserve: Nature enthusiasts will enjoy the calm of Ganavan Sands Nature Reserve, which is a refuge for wildlife and birdwatching. Stroll along the beachfront path, look for seagulls and seals, and appreciate the wildflowers in bloom.

Easdale Island: Take a day excursion to Easdale Island, a hidden gem off the coast of Oban that is only accessible by ferry. Explore the small settlement, stop by the fascinating Easdale Island Folk Museum, and take in the raw beauty of this lonely island.

Off-Beaten Path Attractions

Achnabreck Cup And Ring Marks: Learn about ancient history at Achnabreck Cup and Ring Marks, a lesser-known archaeological site in Kilmartin Glen. Admire the prehistoric rock engravings and ponder their strange origins.

Duart Castle: Travel across the Sound of Mull to discover Duart Castle, an enormous fortification built on a rocky headland overlooking the sea. Discover the castle's rich history, admire its medieval architecture, and enjoy panoramic views from the battlements.

Loch Creran Wildlife Reserve: This reserve is a hidden jewel located between Loch Creran and the surrounding mountains, where you may immerse yourself in nature. Explore the picturesque pathways, sight otters and eagles, and admire the various flora and animals.

Sgurr Dearg: For ambitious hikers looking for a challenge, try Sgurr Dearg, the tallest peak on the Isle of Lismore. Ascend the difficult slopes, scramble across rocky terrain, and be rewarded with spectacular views of the Inner Hebrides from the peak.

Glen Lonan: Discover the serene beauty of Glen Lonan, a remote glen filled with old trees, gushing streams, and hidden waterfalls. Follow the twisting trails, listen to the sounds of nature, and get away from the hurry and bustle of daily life.

Local Dining Secrets

Cuan Mor: Cuan Mor, a hidden gem in the center of Oban, serves fresh fish and handmade beer. Try the catch of the day, hearty pub favorites, and wash it down with a pint of locally made ale.

Ee-Usk: Enjoy great dining with a view at Ee-usk, a seafood restaurant that overlooks Oban Bay. Enjoy fresh oysters, langoustines, and scallops while admiring magnificent views of the bay and neighboring islands.

George Street Fish Restaurant: Enjoy the flavors of Scotland at George Street Fish Restaurant, a family-run establishment noted for its traditional fish and chips. Enjoy wonderfully crispy batter, delicate fish, and handmade tartar sauce, all with a side of pleasant service.

Waterfront Fishouse Restaurant: The Waterfront Fishouse Restaurant, a hidden gem on the banks of Loch Fyne, allows you to dine like a native. Feast on locally sourced delicacies, such as smoked salmon, mussels, and crab, while admiring the breathtaking waterfront views.

Oban Chocolate Company: Satisfy your sweet craving at the Oban Chocolate Company, a local favorite famed for its handcrafted chocolates and gourmet sweets. Browse the delectable collection of truffles, pralines, and fudge, and purchase a box of chocolates as a tasty souvenir.

Insider Recommendations

Take A Wildlife Tour: A guided wildlife tour provides an up-close look at Oban's plentiful wildlife. Join skilled local guides on boat tours or wildlife safaris to see seals, dolphins, whales, and seabirds in their natural habitats.

Attend A Ceilidh: Immerse yourself in Scottish culture and tradition by attending a ceilidh, which is a lively social gathering with traditional music, dancing, and storytelling. Check local listings for ceilidhs held in pubs, community halls, or cultural institutions.

Explore Local Craft Shops: Help local artisans and craftspeople by exploring Oban's lively craft scene. Browse independent boutiques and galleries for handmade jewelry, pottery, textiles, and artwork, and bring home a one-of-a-kind keepsake of your trip to Oban.

Visit Oban Distillery: Take a guided tour of the distillery to learn about the secrets behind Scotch whisky production. Learn about the whisky-making process, drink a variety of single malts, and take in panoramic views of the town from the distillery's visitor center.

Take A Sunset Sail: Enjoy the magic of Oban's sunsets from the water with a sunset sail around the bay. Relax on deck, sip a glass of champagne, and watch the sky turn pink, orange, and gold as the sun sets.

By following these insider suggestions from locals, you'll discover hidden jewels, visit off-the-beaten-path attractions, dine like a local, and acquire unique insights into Oban's culture and lifestyle.

CHAPTER 19

HISTORICAL AND CULTURAL WALKING TOURS

Exploring Oban on foot is a wonderful opportunity to immerse yourself in its rich history and vibrant culture.

In this chapter, we'll take you on four engaging walking tours of Oban, highlighting its historical landmarks, cultural history, and natural beauty. These walking excursions take you from the picturesque alleys of the city center to the rough shoreline and ancient castles, providing a fascinating peek into Oban's heart and soul.

Oban City Walking Tour

Explore Oban's busy city center, where history meets modernity in a beautiful mix of old and new. This walking tour will guide you around Oban's streets and alleyways, introducing you to historic sites, cultural attractions, and hidden jewels.

McCraig's Tower: Start your walking tour at McCraig's Tower, an iconic monument built atop a hill that overlooks the town and port. Built in the nineteenth century by local banker John Stuart McCraig, the tower provides panoramic views of Oban and the surrounding islands.

Oban Distillery: Take a guided tour of the distillery to learn about the secrets behind Scotch whisky production. Learn about the whisky-making process, from malting and mashing to fermentation and distillation, and then taste a variety of exquisite single malts at the end of the tour.

St. John's Cathedral: Explore St. John's Cathedral, a stunning neo-Gothic church in the center of Oban. Learn about its history and relevance to the local community while admiring its gorgeous stained glass windows, complex brickwork, and serene interior.

Oban War And Peace Museum: Step back in time at the Oban War and Peace Museum, which is housed in a former church from the nineteenth century. Explore exhibitions about Oban's maritime history, wartime experiences, and cultural legacy, which include relics, photographs, and interactive displays.

Dunollie Castle: Wrap up your walking trip with a visit to Dunollie Castle, an ancient fortification built on a rocky promontory overlooking the sea. Explore the castle's ruins, which date back to the 12th century, and enjoy panoramic views of Oban Bay and the surrounding shoreline.

Castle And Clan Tour

Explore Oban's medieval past on a castle and clan tour, which delves into the region's rich history of clan warfare, castle construction, and Highland heritage. This walking trip, which includes ancient fortresses and picturesque estates, will transport you back to a bygone era of chieftains and warriors.

Dunstaffnage Castle: Start your visit at Dunstaffnage Castle, one of Scotland's oldest stone castles, which is just a short drive from Oban. Built in the 13th century by the MacDougall clan, the castle served as both a strategic fortification and a royal home.

Dunollie Castle: Continue your journey to Dunollie Castle, the ancestral home of the Clan MacDougall. Explore the ruins of this medieval stronghold, positioned on a rocky promontory with a view of the sea, and hear about its turbulent history and aristocratic inhabitants' traditions.

Duart Castle: Cross the Sound of Mull to see Duart Castle, the ancestral home of the Clan Maclean. This magnificent castle, dating back to the 13th century, is steeped in history and tradition, and offers breathtaking views of the surrounding islands and mainland.

Ardchattan Priory: Discover Ardchattan Priory, a historic priory established in the 13th century by the Valliscaulian order. Discover its calm gardens, historic ruins, and stunning stained glass windows, as well as its significance in medieval Scotland's religious and cultural life.

Kilmartin Glen: Wrap up your journey with a visit to Kilmartin Glen, a hallowed region filled with ancient monuments, standing stones, and burial mounds. Explore the prehistoric sites of Dunadd Fort, Temple Wood Stone Circle, and Nether Largie Standing Stones to learn about Scotland's ancient history.

Whisky Trail Tour

Join a whisky trail tour that showcases Oban's historic whisky producing legacy and the distillers' craftsmanship. From historic distilleries to scenic whisky trails, this walking tour will take you on a trip from grain to glass in the world of Scotch whiskey.

Oban Distillery: Start your whisky trail journey at Oban Distillery, one of Scotland's oldest and most recognizable whisky distilleries. Take a guided tour of the distillery to learn about the whisky-making process, from milling and mashing to fermentation and distillation, and then sample some superb single malts.

Whisky Shop: Visit the whisky shop in Oban's city center, where you'll find a diverse selection of Scotch whiskies, including rare and limited-edition releases. Browse the shelves, speak with expert staff, and purchase a bottle of your favorite whisky to take home as a souvenir.

Coastal Whisky Trail: The coastal whisky route leads around the craggy beaches of Oban Bay, where you'll find magnificent overlooks, hidden coves, and ancient landmarks. Stop along the road to sip a dram of whisky while admiring the stunning seaside views.

Whisky Tasting Experience: Enjoy a whisky tasting in one of Oban's charming pubs or whisky bars. Enjoy a flight of whiskies from various regions of Scotland, experiencing the distinct flavors and smells of each dram while learning about the art of whisky appreciation.

Distillery Tours: Travel beyond Oban to discover other neighboring distilleries on Scotland's whisky path. Visit well-known distilleries on the Isle of Islay, such as Lagavulin, Laphroaig, and Bowmore, or travel to Speyside to explore the legendary whisky distilleries of Glenfiddich, Glenlivet, and Macallan.

Coastal Heritage Tour

Oban's rich maritime history and coastal heritage can be discovered by a walking tour of its gorgeous shoreline, historic harbors, and traditional fishing communities.

This trip emphasizes Oban's deep relationship to the water, including lighthouses, shipwrecks, fishing boats, and seafood markets.

Oban Seaside: Begin your coastal heritage tour on Oban's lovely seaside promenade, which features charming eateries, bustling harbors, and panoramic views of the water. Watch as fishing boats unload their catch for the day and walk along the pier to breathe in the salty sea air.

Dunollie Lighthouse: Explore the Dunollie Lighthouse, a historic beacon set on a rocky outcrop overlooking the entrance to Oban Bay. Built in the nineteenth century to direct ships safely into the harbor, the lighthouse provides breathtaking views of the coastline and adjacent islands.

Oban War Memorial: Pay your respects at the Oban War Memorial, a sad homage to the courageous men and women who have died in conflicts throughout history.

Located on Corran Esplanade, the memorial serves as a somber reminder of the local community's sacrifices.

Ganavan Sands: Take a leisurely stroll along Ganavan Sands, a magnificent stretch of sandy beach located near Oban's town center. Surrounded by steep cliffs and lush trees, this picturesque beach is ideal for a leisurely beachside walk or a picnic with panoramic views.

Puffin Dive Centre: Visit the Puffin Dive Centre to learn about the region's rich marine life and explore its hidden gems through scuba diving and snorkeling trips. Dive among vibrant coral reefs, explore underwater tunnels, and see intriguing aquatic species in their natural environment.

Conclusion: These four walking excursions provide a variety of experiences, allowing you to explore Oban's historical sites, cultural legacy, natural beauty, and maritime traditions on foot.

Oban's intriguing scenery has something for everyone, whether you prefer castle ruins, whisky distilleries, seaside vistas, or marine experiences.

So, put on your walking shoes, grab a map, and begin on an incredible adventure through the heart and spirit of this charming coastal town.

CHAPTER 20

EXPLORING OBAN'S LANDMARK

Oban, with its rich history and breathtaking natural beauty, is home to numerous sites that provide insight into the town's past and present.

From historic castles to modern attractions, each monument reflects Oban's history and cultural significance. In this chapter, we will look at four prominent landmarks that every visitor to Oban should see.

McCaig's Tower

McCaig's Tower, perched on Battery Hill and overlooking Oban, is one of the town's most distinctive sights. Built in the late nineteenth century by local banker John Stuart McCaig, the tower served as both a memorial to his family and a source of income for local stonemasons during the winter.

The edifice, resembling a Roman colosseum, has a series of arches and a central tower that provides panoramic views of Oban Bay and the surrounding islands.

Visitors can ascend the spiral staircase to the summit of the tower, where they will be rewarded with spectacular views over the town, port, and surrounding mountains. The adjacent grounds offer a peaceful respite from the hustle and bustle of the town below, with manicured grass, flower beds, and chairs where visitors may relax and enjoy the view.

McCaig's Tower is especially beautiful at sunset, when the warm colors of the setting sun give a golden glow over the town and bay. It's ideal for photographers, romantics, and anyone looking for a moment of peaceful reflection amidst Oban's breathtaking scenery.

Oban Distillery

No trip to Oban is complete without a tour of Oban Distillery, one of Scotland's oldest and most recognizable whisky distilleries.

The distillery, founded in 1794, has been producing quality single malt Scotch whisky for nearly two centuries, utilizing traditional methods and locally sourced ingredients.

Visitors to Oban Distillery can enjoy a guided tour of the facilities and learn about the entire whisky-making process from beginning to end.

Every stage of the production process, from milling and mashing to fermentation and distillation, is thoroughly explained, providing insight into the art and science of whiskey creation.

The tour culminates with a tasting session, during which guests can try some of Oban's finest whiskies, including the trademark Oban 14-Year-Old single malt. Its rich tastes of honey, citrus, and sea salt perfectly mirror the rugged coastal scenery that surrounds the distillery.

In addition to guided tours, Oban Distillery provides a visitor center and shop where visitors can buy whiskey, souvenirs, and gifts to take home as keepsakes of their trip.

Dunollie Castle

Dunollie Castle, built on a rocky peninsula overlooking Oban Bay, is a medieval fortification steeped in history and folklore. The fortress, which dates back to the 12th century, was formerly the seat of the powerful Clan MacDougall in western Scotland.

Today, Dunollie Castle is in ruins, its aged stone walls bearing witness to centuries of conflict and change. Visitors can visit the castle's remnants, including the magnificent keep, defensive walls, and medieval dwelling quarters, and imagine what life was like for the clansmen who once lived here.

In addition to its historical significance, Dunollie Castle has breathtaking views of Oban Bay and the surrounding shoreline, making it a favorite destination for photographers, hikers, and history buffs alike. A tour to Dunollie Castle provides insight into Scotland's stormy past and the lasting influence of its medieval clans.

Oban War And Peace Museum

The Oban War and Peace Museum, housed in a former church building on Corran Esplanade, is dedicated to preserving memories of Oban's wartime experiences while also promoting modern-day peace and reconciliation.

The museum houses a collection of relics, photographs, and papers about Oban's military history, including displays on World War I, World War II, and the local Home Guard.

Visitors to the museum can view displays about the Battle of the Atlantic, the role of women in combat, and the impact of conflict on the local community. Interactive displays and multimedia presentations shed light on the human cost of war and the significance of learning from the past in order to build a more peaceful future.

In addition to its permanent exhibitions, the Oban War and Peace Museum hosts temporary displays, educational programs, and community events all year. It's a place where people of all ages may learn, reflect, and connect with history in meaningful ways.

These four landmarks provide an insight into Oban's rich heritage, ranging from ancient history to present cultural attractions.

Oban's prominent sites provide something for everyone, whether you're looking to explore old castles, sample exquisite whisky, or learn about the town's military history.

CHAPTER 21

ACCOMMODATION AND DINING DIRECTORIES

Finding the ideal spot to stay and eat is essential for a memorable vacation to Oban.

In this chapter, we'll present extensive directories of popular lodgings, restaurants, cafés, pubs, clubs, and attractions to help you organize your trip effectively.

Addresses And Locations For Popular Accommodation

Oban Bay Hotel And Spa

Address: Corran Esplanade, Oban, Argyll, PA34 5AE.

Description: This hotel, located on the waterfront, provides exquisite accommodations with spa amenities as well as spectacular views of Oban Bay.

The Perle Oban Hotel

Address: Station Square, Oban, Argyll, PA34 5RT.

Description: Located in the heart of Oban, this boutique hotel offers elegant rooms, a restaurant, and a cocktail bar.

The Regent Hotel

Address: Corran Esplanade, Oban, Argyll, PA34 5PZ.

Description: A family-run hotel facing the bay with pleasant accommodations, a restaurant serving Scottish cuisine, and a quiet bar.

Columba Hotel

Address: North Pier, Oban, Argyll, PA34 5QD.

Description: Located near the ferry terminal, this historic hotel has exquisite rooms, a restaurant, and a lounge with panoramic views of the bay.

Lagganbeg Guesthouse

Address: Gallanach Road, Oban, Argyll, PA34 4EG.

Description: A beautiful guesthouse overlooking the waterfront with pleasant rooms and a kind Scottish welcome.

Addresses And Locations Of Popular Restaurants And Cafés

EE-Usk

Address: Gallanach Road, Oban, Argyll, PA34 4LS.

Description: A seafood restaurant on the waterfront noted for its fresh seafood dishes and spectacular bay views.

Coast Restaurant

Address: George Street, Oban, Argyll, PA34 5RX.

Description: A modern restaurant with locally sourced seafood and Scottish cuisine in a trendy atmosphere.

Cuán Mor

Address: George Street, Oban, Argyll, PA34 5NX.

Description: A vibrant gastropub with a broad menu including pub classics, craft brews, and live music events.

Piazza

Address: Stafford Street, Oban, Argyll, PA34 5NJ.

Description: An Italian restaurant and café that serves wood-fired pizzas, pasta meals, and gelato desserts in a relaxing setting.

Oban Chocolate Company

Address: Corran Esplanade, Oban, Argyll, PA34 5PS.

Description: A beautiful café and chocolatier that serves handmade chocolates, cakes, and hot drinks while overlooking the bay.

Addresses And locations Of Popular Bars And Clubs

Markie Dans

Address: 2 Victoria Crescent, Oban, Argyll, PA34 5DX.

Description: A classic Scottish bar with a comfortable environment that serves whiskey, beers, and pub food.

The Lorne Bar

Address: Stevenson Street, Oban, Argyll, PA 34 5NA

Description: A welcoming neighborhood bar known for live music, quiz nights, and a diverse drink menu.

Cuán Mor Bar

Address: George Street, Oban, Argyll, PA34 5NX.

Description: Cuan Mor's bar serves a variety of artisan beers, drinks, and spirits.

Corran Halls

Address: Corran Esplanade, Oban, Argyll, PA34 5AB.

Description: A multi-purpose venue that hosts live music, comedy shows, and club nights while overlooking Oban Bay.

Lorne Bar

Address: Stevenson Street, Oban, Argyll, PA 34 5NA

Description: A classic Scottish bar with a casual environment that serves whiskey, beers, and substantial pub fare.

Addresses And Locations Of Major Attractions

Oban Distillery

Address: Stafford Street, Oban, Argyll, PA 34 5NH

Description: Join a guided tour of the Oban Distillery to learn about the whisky-making process and drink a variety of superb single malts.

Dunollie Castle

Address: Dunollie Road, Oban, Argyll, PA34 5TT.

Description: Explore the ruins of this medieval fortress, which offers panoramic views of Oban Bay and the surrounding shoreline.

McCaig's Tower

Address: Battery Hill, Oban, Argyll, PA34 5DP.

Description: Climb to the summit of this iconic monument to enjoy panoramic views over Oban Bay, the town, and the surrounding islands.

Oban War And Peace Museum

Address: Corran Esplanade, Oban, Argyll, PA34 5PX.

Description: Discover Oban's wartime experiences, as well as the local community's attempts to promote peace and reconciliation.

Oban Sealife Sanctuary

Address: Dunollie Road, Oban, Argyll, PA34 5TT.

Description: Visit the Oban Sea Life Sanctuary to see Scotland's diverse marine life, including seals, otters, sharks, and other intriguing creatures.

McCaig's Tower

Address: Battery Hill, Oban, Argyll, PA34 5DP.

Description: This renowned landmark offers panoramic views of Oban Bay, the town, and the surrounding islands.

Oban Chocolate Company

Address: Corran Esplanade, Oban, Argyll, PA34 5PS.

Description: Indulge your sweet craving at this beautiful café and chocolatier, which serves handmade chocolates, cakes, and hot drinks.

Ganavan Sands

Address: Ganavan Road, Oban, Argyll, PA34 5TU.

Description: Take a leisurely stroll or picnic on this gorgeous sandy beach, which offers breathtaking views of the coastline and surrounding islands.

Dunstaffnage Castle & Chapel

Address: Dunbeg, Oban, Argyll, PA37 1PZ.

Description: Explore the ruins of this medieval castle from the 13th century, as well as the adjoining chapel, which is one of Scotland's oldest stone structures.

Oban Phoenix Cinema

Address: George Street, Oban, Argyll, PA34 5NX.

Description: For a one-of-a-kind cinematic experience, visit this lovely independent cinema located in a former church.

These top sites provide a varied range of experiences, including historic landmarks, natural marvels, cultural venues, and culinary pleasures.

CHAPTER 22

CONCLUSION

As your stay in Oban comes to an end, it's time to reflect on the memorable experiences you've had, appreciate the memories you've created, and say goodbye to this charming seaside town.

In this final chapter, we'll reflect on your Oban trip, look at some farewell rituals, talk about your future adventure, and depart Oban with memories to treasure.

Reflecting On Your Oban Experience

As you prepare to leave Oban, take a minute to think on the many experiences you've had here. Perhaps you've seen historic castles, enjoyed wonderful seafood, gone on outdoor excursions, or simply admired the gorgeous countryside.

Consider the memories that have stayed with you, the sights and sounds that have moved you, and the ties you've formed with the people and places of Oban.

Oban has surely left an impression on you, from its rocky shoreline to its locals' friendly hospitality. Whether you spend a few days or a few weeks exploring its wonders, the experiences you made here will last long after you leave.

Farewell Traditions In Oban

In Oban, saying goodbye is frequently accompanied with time-honored traditions reflecting the town's rich history and legacy. One such custom is the lighting of the "Farewell Fire," which is a symbolic gesture of saying goodbye to visitors and wishing them safe journeys back home.

This ritual is commonly carried out on the shores of Oban Bay, where locals and visitors come to watch the flames dance against the backdrop of the setting sun.

Another farewell ritual in Oban is to share "Drambuie," a traditional Scottish beverage made from whiskey, honey, herbs, and spices. This sweet and aromatic beverage is frequently served as a show of hospitality and kindness, representing friendship and camaraderie. Sharing a toast with newfound friends or fellow tourists is an appropriate way to conclude your time in Oban and commemorate the memories you've created together.

Plan Your Next Adventure

As you say goodbye to Oban, it's normal to begin thinking about your next trip. Perhaps you've discovered a new love of outdoor adventure, a taste for Scottish cuisine, or a drive to learn more about Scotland's rich history and culture.

Use your time in Oban to plan your next trip, whether it's exploring other coastal communities along Scotland's west coast, venturing further into the country's highlands and islands, or beginning on a new adventure in a far-flung location. Allow the experiences you created in Oban to feed your wanderlust and guide you on your next adventure.

Leave Oban With Memories To Cherish

As you depart Oban, take a moment to reflect on the memories you've made here.

Remember the laughs you had with friends, the excursions you went on, and the peaceful moments you spent admiring the beauty of Oban's natural surroundings. As you continue your journey, keep these memories in mind as a reminder of the kindness and generosity you received in this coastal refuge.

As you say goodbye to Oban, remember that you're departing with more than just memories; you're taking a portion of its soul, beauty, and charm. Until we meet again, may your journeys be full with adventure, discovery, and the excitement of new experiences.

As you conclude your stay in Oban, may the memories you've created here continue to inspire and enrich your life's journey.

Farewell, Oban, until we meet again.

CHAPTER 23

APPENDIX

This appendix contains a number of useful resources to help you make the most of your trip to Oban.

These resources, which include emergency contact information, maps and navigational tools, further reading and references, and important local words, can assist ensure a smooth and pleasurable visit.

Emergency Contacts

Emergency Services: For emergencies, including police, fire, and medical assistance, dial 999.

Oban Police Station

Address: Albany Street, Oban, Argyll, PA34 4AR

Phone: 101 (non-emergency)

Oban Hospital

Address: Glengallan Road, Oban, Argyll, PA34 4HH

Phone: +44 (0) 1631 567500

Coastguard

Phone: 999 or 112

Mountain Rescue

Phone: 999 or 112

Maps And Navigational Tools

Google Maps (www.maps.google.com): Google Maps provides precise maps and directions to help you navigate Oban and the surrounding area.

You may also use it to locate nearby attractions, restaurants, and lodging.

Visit Scotland Interactive Map:

www.visitscotland.com/maps: Use interactive maps of Scotland, including Oban, to find places of interest, beautiful routes, and travel suggestions.

Oban Town Map: Get a physical copy of the Oban town map from the local tourist information center or hotel. It gives a full description of the town's layout, including major attractions and areas of interest.

Additional Reading And References

Oban Tourist Information Centre website:

www.oban.org.uk: The Oban Tourist Information Center's official website contains a variety of information about attractions, events, lodgings, and other topics.

VisitScotland (www.visitscotland.com): The VisitScotland website offers extensive travel guides, itineraries, and tips for experiencing Scotland, including Oban.

Lonely Planet Scotland

The Lonely Planet guidebook to Scotland contains full information about Oban, including recommendations for lodging, restaurants, activities, and more.

Historic Environment Scotland

www.historicenvironment.scot: Discover Scotland's rich history and legacy, including the historic sites and landmarks in and around Oban.

Useful Local Phrases

"Slàinte Mhath!" (Slan-Ge-Var): Cheers! (Literally translates to "good health!")

"Ciamar A Tha Sibh?" (Kee-Mar A Ha Shee-v): How are you?

"Tapadh Leibh" (Ta-Pa Layv): Thank you (formal).

"Feasgar Math" (Fes-Ker Mah): Good afternoon.

"Fàilte Gu Oban" (Fal-Che Gue Oh-Ban): Welcome to Oban.

"Ceud Mìle Fàilte" (K-Yu-Mee-Le Fal-Che): A hundred thousand welcomes.

Remember to use these phrases to welcome locals and express your gratitude for their hospitality throughout your trip to Oban.

Addresses And Locations Of Popular Accommodation

The Royal Hotel Oban

Address: Argyll Square, Oban, Argyll, PA34 4BE

Website: www.royalhotel-oban.com

The Regent Hotel

Address: Corran Esplanade, Oban, Argyll, PA34 5PZ

Website: www.regenthoteloban.co.uk

Columba Hotel

Address: North Pier, Oban, Argyll, PA34 5QD

Website: www.columbahoteloban.co.uk

Oban Bay Hotel

Address: Corran Esplanade, Oban, Argyll, PA34 5AE

Website: www.crerarhotels.com/oban-bay-hotel

The Ranald Hotel

Address: 41 Stevenson Street, Oban, Argyll, PA34 5NA

Website: www.theranaldhotel.com

Addresses And Locations Of Popular Restaurants And Cafés

EE-Usk

Address: North Pier, Oban, Argyll, PA34 5QD

Website: www.eeusk.com

Café Spice

Address: 10 Argyll Square, Oban, Argyll, PA34 4AZ

Website: www.cafespiceoban.co.uk

Piazza Italian Restaurant

Address: 4 Stafford Street, Oban, Argyll, PA34 5NJ

Website: www.piazzaitalianrestaurant.co.uk

Cuan Mor

Address: 55 George Street, Oban, Argyll, PA34 5DS

Website: www.cuanmor.co.uk

Oban Chocolate Company Café

Address: Corran Esplanade, Oban, Argyll, PA34 5PS

Website: www.obanchocolate.co.uk

Addresses And Locations Of Popular Bars And Clubs

The Oban Inn

Address: 22 Stafford Street, Oban, Argyll, PA34 5NJ

Website: www.obaninn.com

Markie Dans

Address: 2 Craigard Road, Oban, Argyll, PA34 5NP

Website: www.markiedans.com

Aulay's Bar

Address: 8 Airds Crescent, Oban, Argyll, PA34 5SQ

Website: www.aulays.com

The Lorne Bar

Address: 57 George Street, Oban, Argyll, PA34 5DS

Website: www.lorneoban.co.uk

Corryvreckan Whisky Bar

Address: 1 Stafford Street, Oban, Argyll, PA34 5NH

Website: www.corryvreckanwhisky.com

Addresses And Locations Of Top Attractions

McCaig's Tower

Address: Battery Hill, Oban, Argyll, PA34 5DP

Oban Distillery

Address: Stafford Street, Oban, Argyll, PA34 5NH

Website: www.obanwhisky.com

Dunollie Castle

Address: Dunollie Road, Oban, Argyll, PA34 5TT

Website: www.dunollie.org

Oban War And Peace Museum

Address: Corran Esplanade, Oban, Argyll, PA34 5PX

Website: www.obantown.org.uk/museum

Ganavan Sands

Address: Ganavan Road, Oban, Argyll, PA34 5TU

These addresses and locations will take you to some of Oban's most popular hotels, restaurants, bars, clubs, and attractions. Enjoy touring this stunning seaside village!

MAPS

Oban Scotland

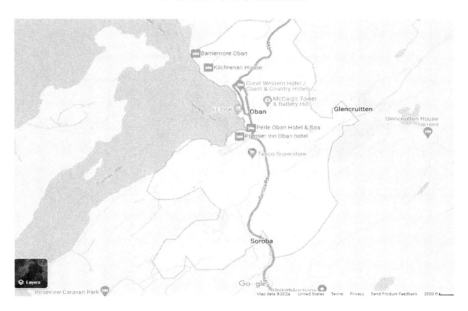

https://maps.app.goo.gl/8uM6trkJmamRy5dbA

USE YOUR PHONE TO SCAN THE QR CODE IMAGE TO GET THE LOCATIONS IN REAL TIME

Things To Do In Oban

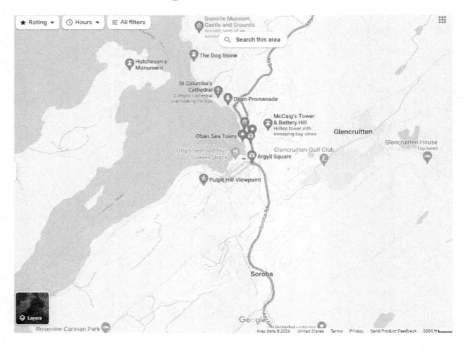

https://maps.app.goo.gl/LSndjsuewAnrFxoKA

USE YOUR PHONE TO SCAN THE QR CODE IMAGE TO GET THE LOCATIONS IN REAL TIME

Hotels In Oban

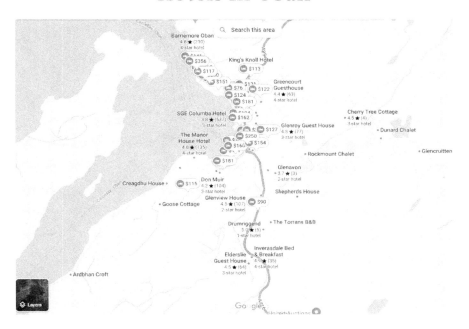

https://maps.app.goo.gl/ZavV8iBxQZ6Ed2vJ7

USE YOUR PHONE TO SCAN THE QR CODE IMAGE TO GET THE LOCATIONS IN REAL TIME

Vacation Rentals

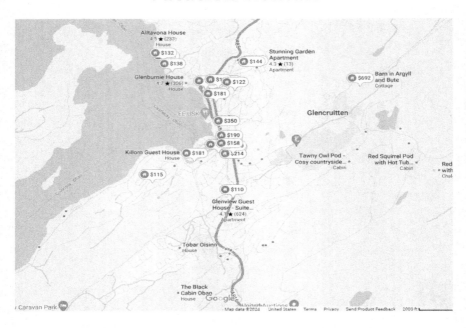

https://maps.app.goo.gl/1aEzKfdA5k3Q2cDbA

USE YOUR PHONE TO SCAN THE QR CODE IMAGE TO GET THE LOCATIONS IN REAL TIME

Restaurants In Oban

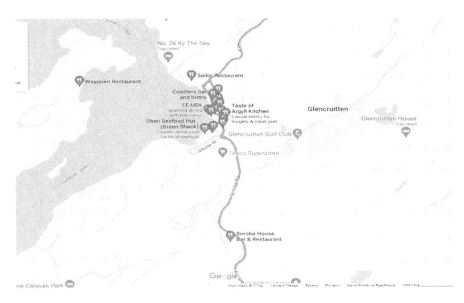

https://maps.app.goo.gl/3oivJ3578aybJhEs7

USE YOUR PHONE TO SCAN THE QR CODE IMAGE TO GET THE LOCATIONS IN REAL TIME

Museums In Oban

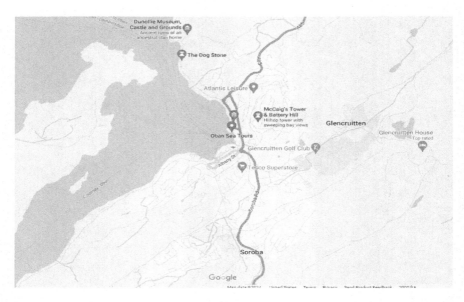

https://maps.app.goo.gl/LYTTVw8NZQeWAgdU8

USE YOUR PHONE TO SCAN THE QR CODE IMAGE TO GET THE LOCATIONS IN REAL TIME

Pharmacies In Oban

https://maps.app.goo.gl/vS67MkBJWM49TJY2A

USE YOUR PHONE TO SCAN THE
QR CODE IMAGE TO GET THE
LOCATIONS IN REAL TIME

ATMs In Oban

https://maps.app.goo.gl/PP1sBjrMaQCe8bea8

USE YOUR PHONE TO SCAN THE
QR CODE IMAGE TO GET THE
LOCATIONS IN REAL TIME

Streets In Oban

https://www.openstreetmap.org/#map=15/56.4108/-5.4669

USE YOUR PHONE TO SCAN THE QR CODE IMAGE TO GET THE LOCATIONS IN REAL TIME

Streets In Oban

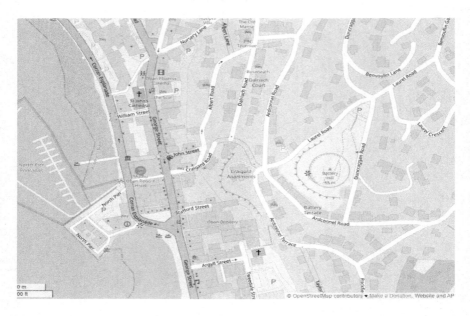

https://www.openstreetmap.org/#map=17/56.41580/-5.47116

USE YOUR PHONE TO SCAN THE
QR CODE IMAGE TO GET THE
LOCATIONS IN REAL TIME

Hiking Trails In Oban

https://maps.app.goo.gl/2HFdzVrtpBSdhotv5

USE YOUR PHONE TO SCAN THE QR CODE IMAGE TO GET THE LOCATIONS IN REAL TIME

IMAGE ATTRIBUTION

https://pixabay.com/photos/scotland-oban-port-ship-4496962/
(Cover page)

APPRECIATION

Thank you so much for purchasing **Kiera Clayton's Travel Guide**! I truly appreciate your support and hope this guide helps you create amazing memories on your journey. Your feedback means the world to me, so if you found this book helpful, I would love it if you could take a moment to leave a review. Your thoughts not only help me improve, but also assist other travelers in planning their perfect trip. Thank you again, and happy travels!

Printed in Dunstable, United Kingdom